150 Things to Know Now That You're a Grownup

SHAWN CORNELIUS

Published by Yukon Publishing
Strongsville, Ohio
www.yukonpublishing.com

Cover by Brad Fagan

Special discounts are available on purchases of bulk quantities.
For more information please contact the publisher
at info@yukonpublishing.com.

ISBN-13: 978-0-9982672-0-3

DEDICATION

To my wife, Suzanne, for her unrelenting support; and to my kids, Kristen, Sydney, and Matthew for giving me a reason to write this book.

CONTENTS

FOREWORD.. 6

INTRODUCTION 9

MONEY 11
Personal Finance in a Nutshell.................................... 12
Budgets: The King of Personal Finance............................. 15
Assets and Debts: Two Sides of the Same Coin 25
Cash Flow: Lubrication to Keep it Running...................... 35
Risk Management: Protect for the Unexpected 45
Savings: Converting Income to Assets 59
Investing: Making Your Money Work............................. 70
Credit Cards: Friend and Foe....................................... 85
Taxes: Uncle Sam's Piece of the Pie.................................. 91
Buying vs Renting: The Tradeoffs................................. 99
Outsourcing: Time is Money....................................... 104

CAREER..107
The Work: Doing It Right 108
Your Boss: Becoming Successful Together 131
Managing Expectations: Baselines Matter.......................... 142
The Workplace: Keeping it Professional............................ 148
Professional Relationships: Required for Success............. 153
Communication: The Life-Blood of Business.................. 161
Negotiation: Science, not Art 170
Management and Leadership: It's About People 176
Job Security: Your Job, Your Problem 185

TRAVEL...195
Travel Rewards: Membership has its Privileges 196
Air Travel: Tricks of the Trade 200
Hotels: Feeling at Home 205

HOUSES.. 209
House Expenses: Where Most of Your Money Goes...... 210
House Maintenance: An Ounce of Prevention 215

House Issues: A Pound of Cure 222

CARS **231**
Car Expenses: The Purchase is Just the Beginning 232
Car Maintenance: Protecting your Investment 238
Car Issues: When Things Go Wrong 245

THE FULL LIST **251**

ACKNOWLEDGMENTS **257**

INDEX **258**

FOREWORD

Shortly after my daughter, Kristen, graduated from college, she came to me with a peculiar request, "Dad, you need to teach me what I need to know to be a grownup."

Confused, I asked her what she meant. Then she unleashed a flood of questions. The questions weren't abstract or philosophical; they were practical questions about how mortgages work, what insurance she needed, whether she should buy a house, and how to be successful at work.

That's how this book came to be.

The perspectives in this book are mine. I'm not a financial planner, nor a lawyer, travel agent, real-estate developer, or auto mechanic. I'm just a dad, who's experienced some success in my personal life and in business via the lessons learned in this book. You may not agree with everything that's written within these pages, and that's ok. At a minimum, I hope it sparks some thought about the topics within.

Also, since the content of this book is based on my experiences, there is a natural bias towards what I know. In particular, much of what's written here presumes a US audience and/or work in a business related field. I'm hopeful that international readers or those working in other fields will still find the concepts useful.

Lastly, this is a book of practical advice. Certainly understanding personal finance and how to change a tire does not make one a grownup. I leave the larger emotional, behavioral, and spiritual questions of what it means to act like an adult to other capable authors.

If you have any feedback on the topics within this book, or have other topics you'd like to see in a future publication, please feel free to contact me at shawn.cornelius@yukonpublishing.com.

Shawn Cornelius
First-time Author, Long-time Dad

INTRODUCTION

This book will not teach you to be a grownup. You'll learn to be a grownup the same way we all have; you'll try things and be successful; you'll try things and fail; and you'll collect life experiences along the way.

But hopefully this book will give you a head start.

Captured in these pages is a sampling of my life experiences and lessons learned from a lifetime of successes and failures. Some of them may apply to you more than others, and some of them may not apply at all.

The main part of this book is broken up into five sections, covering Money, Career, Travel, Houses, and Cars. Each of those sections is then divided into groupings of things you need to know. Finally, at the back of the book you'll find the full list of the 150 Things to Know.

I hope you enjoy reading this book as much as I enjoyed writing it.

MONEY

Now that you're a grownup with a real job, it's time to get organized around your finances. There's a lot to it; but the good news is that you can put some structure around it to make it manageable.

PERSONAL FINANCE IN A NUTSHELL

1

Personal finance has four parts

Corporations manage and report their financials on three main accounting documents:

- The **Income Statement** illustrates the profitability of a company by capturing the revenue over a given time period (like a specific quarter or year) and the expenses over that same time period. The difference between these numbers is profit.

- The **Balance Sheet** captures at a point in time all of a company's assets (what they own) and all of the company's liabilities (what they owe). This is effectively what the company is worth if it stopped operating.

- The **Statement of Cash Flows** shows how much money has come in and how much money has gone out over a given time period. It's not the same as the Income Statement, in part because there is a difference between when the revenue and expense is incurred and when the money (cash) actually changes hands.

This model fits very nicely with a model for personal finance:

- A **Budget** is the personal equivalent of an Income Statement, detailing what income is coming in (or planned to come in) and what costs are going out (or planned to go out).

- **Assets and Debts** is the personal equivalent of a Balance Sheet, detailing the value of what you own, and the value of debt you owe. The difference between what you own and what you owe is Net Worth.

- **Cash Flow** is the personal equivalent of the Statement of Cash Flows. It shows how much cash has come in and gone out. In personal finance, it will typically differ from the Budget because of the timing of when you buy something vs when you pay for it. For example, you may buy something on a credit card in March that fits within your March budget, but not have enough cash in your bank account in May when that credit card bill comes due to pay for that purchase. Or you may have a balanced budget, but the timing of the bills doesn't match well with when you receive your paychecks, so when the bills hit you don't have the cash to pay them.

There is a fourth element of personal finance that is critically important. It's also a component of corporate finance, but it's managed outside of the three main accounting documents. **Risk Management** is where you protect your finances from unexpected events. This is where insurance plays a key role.

What you need to know for each of the four key parts of personal finance; Budgets, Assets and Debts, Cash Flow, and Risk Management; are captured in the following sections.

BUDGETS:
THE KING OF
PERSONAL FINANCE

2

A monthly budget is your most important financial tool

Budgets serve a few important purposes:

- They help you with financial planning
- They help you restrain your spending
- They help you track your spending

From a planning perspective, your budget is the tool you use to make decisions around how you are going to spend your money. Are you going to spend more money at Starbucks or put more money into your savings account? It's easier to make these decisions ahead of time on paper, than rely on yourself making the best decision real time.

From a restraint perspective, your budget will at least make you think about your spending when you are in the process of spending your hard earned money. But a budget is like a diet; if you try and stick too closely to it, you'll just end up feeling frustrated and ashamed when you overrun it. So think of your budget as a guideline; a way to implement your financial strategies day-to-day. If you overrun it once in a while, it's ok. If you are overrunning it every month, it's time to redo the budget.

From a tracking perspective, your budget will shine light on where your hard earned cash is going. I spend how much a month on Chipotle?! These insights may lead you to cut back your spending in certain areas, or it may lead you to make adjustments to your budget.

Budgets help you plan, restrain, and track your spending. If you only implement one financial tool, make sure that tool is a monthly budget.

3

Creating a monthly budget is easy

In the old days, budgets were a bear to create and keep up with. You had to create a spreadsheet, slog through all of your transactions, put them all into categories, etc. Now there are online tools (my favorite is www.mint.com) that amongst other things, help you set a budget and track against that budget by integrating with your bank and credit cards and automatically categorizing the transactions for you.

The most effective way to create and live within your budget is to start with what you are currently spending in each category, and then make adjustments to how much you'd like to spend in each category. On-line tools significantly accelerate this process.

Creating a monthly budget is easy and well worth it.

4

Your monthly budget should balance

It's very important that your monthly budget balances. Balancing the budget means making the income minus expenses equal zero (or be really close to zero).

If your expenses exceed your income, you are living above your means and detracting from your net worth. This isn't sustainable! If your budget is in negative territory, you need to make changes in terms of reducing expenses or increasing your income.

While not as serious a problem, it's also an issue if you have a large surplus in your monthly budget. A large surplus is a missed opportunity to invest more in savings. Left in your checking account, you're more likely to spend it frivolously and less likely to get a good return on the money. Of course, your monthly budget will always be off by a little bit – it's only large surpluses that are a concern.

Get in the habit early of setting up a balanced budget and sticking to it.

5

You need to budget for savings

Saving money doesn't just happen. You need to budget putting the money away. Going even further, you should set up an automatic transfer from your checking account to savings accounts every month for the budgeted amount, to ensure that your savings is staying on budget.

Most Americans are pretty terrible at saving. In 2015, Americans under the age of 35 put away an average of <u>negative</u> 1.8% of their income. Americans 35-44 saved an average of 2.6% while those aged 45-54 saved an average of 5.7% of their income[1]. Keep in mind that this is across all savings accounts, including retirement! By contrast, in our household, we save 20-25% of our after-tax income.

You should budget as much for savings as you possibly can. Your balanced budget will feel tight, but you can feel good about it, knowing that it's tight because you are maximizing how much you are saving!

---

[1] Source: Moody Analytics via The Wall Street Journal, Census Bureau, 2015

6

It's easiest to save the money you never see

Whenever you get a raise or some unexpected money comes in (like a bonus), consider first putting some or all of it away. Since you never had the money prior, it won't feel like as much of a sacrifice; you'll still be able to maintain your same standard of living as before.

In our household, we've consistently used a "50/50" rule for any unexpected windfalls (like bonuses); 50% immediately went to savings, and 50% went to something else (like house projects, vacations, etc.). This way we could feel good about socking a good chunk of money away while still celebrating the windfall.

Save the money before you see it!

7

You will spend what you make

The reason why it's so important to have a balanced budget and budget for savings (especially the money you never see), is because you will always spend what you make. It's a universal rule that's really hard to understand when you are starting out, but trust me. Today, what seems like a lot of money to you, won't be a lot of money to you ten years from now. Your financial frame-of-reference always changes with your income.

8

Budgets are evergreen

Because both your income and expenses change periodically, your budget will always need to be updated. Quarterly reviews are ideal. Your income may not change that fast, but looking at your budget quarterly will force you to revisit how you are spending your money, and make adjustments.

9

You should periodically review recurring payments

Your budget will usually contain a handful of providers that you pay consistently every month for a service. This includes companies that provide:

- Cable TV/Internet
- Utility (Electric, Gas, Water, Sewer)
- Insurance
- Mobile Phone Service

Because these companies provide an ongoing service, it's easy to become comfortable with paying them every month. These providers know this, so they don't go out of their way to stay price competitive. They may periodically raise rates on you; or at a minimum, they aren't going to lower the price or offer special deals when they are fighting off the competition. For example, if AT&T, Sprint, and Verizon are in a price-war, you're unlikely to see the benefits of that unless you are a new customer, or you reach out to the provider.

Therefore, it makes sense to periodically look at your recurring expenses and see if you can get the service cheaper. Many times, you don't even have to switch providers, you just need to call them and threaten to leave.

ASSETS AND DEBTS: TWO SIDES OF THE SAME COIN

10

Assets are thought of in terms of risk and return

An asset is something you own. It could be something physical like a house, a car, or baseball cards. It could also be something less tangible like a share of a company's profits (stock) or a promise of interest paid (bond).

All assets are investments, and the most fundamental aspect of investing is risk and return. Return is the payback you expect to get back from the investment (usually expressed as a percentage of what you paid for it). Risk is a qualitative measure of how likely it is that you'll get the return that you expect.

For example, playing the lottery is extremely high risk and extremely high return. Investing $1.00 on a lottery ticket may return $60,000,000, but the chances of it returning that are near zero. At the other extreme, investing $1.00 in a savings account at your local bank might return just 1%, or 1 penny per year, but since it's insured by the US Government, which is unlikely to disappear anytime soon, it is extremely low risk. Generally speaking, risk and return are directly related. If an investment is risky, the only way people will buy it is because it has a high potential return. Likewise, if an investment has a low potential return, investors aren't willing to incur a lot of risk.

Also, some assets have zero or even a negative return, and we might be ok with that. For example, cars depreciate in value very quickly; but we don't buy cars for their investment potential, we buy them to transport ourselves around town. So for cars and other household things we use, we don't really include them as investments for the purpose of financial planning.

For any asset that is exists primarily as an investment, it is always useful to think of it in terms of risk and return.

11

Debt is neither good nor bad

This statement might surprise you and some people might even consider it controversial; but debt is not a bad thing.

Consider this. If you could borrow money from a bank at 3% and use it to purchase an investment that guaranteed a 6% return a year, would you do it? Of course. You would borrow every penny the bank would lend you.

Unfortunately, it's never quite that straight forward, primarily because all investments have risk, and risk and return are directly correlated so such an obvious discrepancy between the rate at the bank and the return on a guaranteed investment doesn't happen very often. But it does happen in subtler ways. Consider buying a house, where the housing market is growing at 4% appreciation, mortgage rates are at 5%, and the US Government considers mortgage interest tax deductible. Indeed, this is a real scenario where debt becomes what investors call "leverage".

Financial leverage refers to using borrowed money in an investment, with the expectation that the profits from the investment will be greater than the interest you pay to borrow the money. In the mortgage example above, the effective interest rate you pay to the bank (after the government gives you a tax break) is less than what you would reasonably expect in terms of appreciation on your house's value.

While debt is inherently neither good nor bad, debt can be very bad. In fact, it can be devastating. At some point, if you incur too much debt (or the wrong kind of debt), you won't be able to keep up with the payments; and there is no easy way to recover once you fall behind.

The important thing is to recognize that debt is just a tool. Used intelligently it can be very valuable. Used foolishly, it can lead to financial catastrophe.

12

You should consider assets and debts as a portfolio

Since both debts and assets come in all kinds of flavors, it's best to think of all of them in a single portfolio (a collection) and manage them as such. You don't want all low return investments; nor do you want all high risk investments. You want a mix.

To the extent that you have debt, you should also consider this in your overall portfolio. Of course, you want the lowest interest rate possible on your debt, but thinking about debt as a part of your overall portfolio will help you see the tradeoffs between your debts and investments. This is important because when you have extra cash, that money could go to reducing debt, or it could go to increasing investment. Looking at both debts and assets in the same portfolio can help with the decision.

13

Financial decisions are about balancing risk and return

The point of considering all of your debts and assets in a single portfolio is so that you can more easily make decisions around financial tradeoffs.

For example, are you better off:

- Paying off your student loan or putting more to your retirement?
- Paying off your credit card or your student loan?
- Selling your savings bonds to pay off your student loans?
- Renting an apartment or taking a loan to buy a house?
- Putting your bonus towards retirement or in your savings account?

There are many considerations in these decisions besides financial, but from a financial perspective they all come down to risk and return.

Comparing assets is usually fairly straightforward. If the stock market is high risk but pays 11% a year on average, and your savings account is very low risk but pays 1% a year on average;

you can compare these two options in the context of how much risk you are willing to take on; how much risk you already have in the portfolio; and how long you have until you need the money (because the longer the time frame, the more time you have to recover if the return goes south).

It's less intuitive, but you can also compare debts and assets in the same way. Most of your debt will likely have a fixed interest rate, in which case it effectively has zero risk – the rate is the rate is the rate. Some debt instruments are variable and do have a risk associated with the rate going up. Either way, comparing assets and debts is the same as comparing assets to assets.

Consider this. What is the difference in putting $100 towards an investment that returns 2% a year vs putting $100 towards a loan with an interest rate of 2% a year? Of course the financial impact is exactly the same. In the first case you earn $2.00 and in the second case you save $2.00. Either way, you are better off by two dollars.

When you make financial decisions, it is wise to always anchor back to the fundamental concepts of risk and return.

14

The liquidity of assets varies widely

There is one other critically important consideration as it relates to assets. Liquidity refers to the ability to turn the asset into cash that you can actually spend. An asset that is very liquid (like cash or money in your savings account) can be accessed and spent quickly. An asset that is not very liquid (like a 401(k) or physical property like your house) cannot easily be turned into money that you can spend.

Liquidity only really matters if you need to get the money out of the asset (i.e. "liquidate", or sell the asset). This does become a consideration when you are saving for large purchases. For example, you generally wouldn't plan on putting a bunch of extra money into your retirement account in hopes of using the money to buy a house in a year. Your retirement account wouldn't be considered very liquid. (That said, there are mechanisms that allow you to liquidate part of your retirement account for special circumstances like buying a house via a 401(k) loan, but that's a fairly circuitous way to save for a house).

Keep liquidity in mind with your financial planning.

15

Your credit report matters

Your credit report tells lenders how creditworthy you are. Lenders use your credit score from your credit report to determine whether they should issue you a loan and what interest rate they should provide you. The better your credit score, the less risk there is to the lender, and therefore the more willing they are to give you a lower rate.

Federal law allows you to get a copy of your credit report every 12 months for free (otherwise you can pay for a copy). You can go on-line to access your report.

You should review your credit report at least once a year to ensure:

- There are no mistakes in your report in terms of incorrectly reported late payments, missed payments, etc. If there are mistakes, you need to contact the credit agency that provides the report.
- There are no credit cards, loans, or addresses on your report that you don't recognize. This is a clear indicator of identity theft. If this happens, contact the credit agency and the police.

CASH FLOW: LUBRICATION TO KEEP IT RUNNING

16

You need multiple checking and saving accounts

You're probably used to having one checking account and one savings account. But as your financial situation changes, you will find you need multiple accounts to keep things straight. Opening additional accounts is easy, and many adults have multiple accounts.

Reasons for having multiple accounts include:

- separating accounts so you and your spouse can each track their own spending
- saving for multiple purposes
- enforcing saving or spending discipline
- convenience in separating out financials

The two things that married couples fight the most about are money and kids. On the money front, it's challenging to take two independent people and come up with a system for paying the bills. Sometimes one person pays all of the bills out of a central account. The challenge is that the other person therefore doesn't know what's going on in the account, so if they want to spend money they either have to ask their spouse or spend the money and hope it fits in the budget (and cash flow). Or you can get into the realm of one spouse receiving a "spending allowance", which can create other issues of control.

I've found that the best model is to have separate checking accounts, with each account servicing a different part of the budget with a different income stream (or a set monthly transfer from one account to the other). Each spouse controls one of the two accounts, which gives each person some flexibility with regards to budgeting and spending. Of course, no one system works for everyone.

From a saving perspective, you will have multiple savings goals. You may be simultaneously saving for a down payment on a house, a car, a vacation, college, or retirement. Having separate savings vehicles will help you track against each of those goals.

In addition to the convenience of keeping some of your financial concerns separate from one another, it also helps you stay disciplined. You can set up automatic transfers between accounts to force saving or you can simply have accounts allocated to a single use, so you aren't tempted to use that money for a different purpose.

17

Business expenses should stay separate

Nothing will screw up your personal financials faster than intermingling your personal expense and income with business expense and reimbursement.

The problem looks like this. For several months, you're traveling for work, charging in a few thousand dollars in expenses every month, and every month getting a reimbursement to fully cover the expenses. At the end of several months, you stop traveling and stop getting the expense reimbursement. But somehow you still have a few thousand dollars left on your credit card. How did that happen?! Well, over those several months you were inadvertently using some of your expense reimbursement money for other things. It was imperceptible each month, until at the end you find yourself with a shortfall!

Therefore, it's important to keep a separate credit card and separate checking account for your business expenses.

18

Automatic payments are your friend

Wherever possible, you should set up your bills to be automatically paid in full each month from your checking account. This will save you the time of having to track your bills and write the checks (or pay online), plus it will remove any tendency to short-pay your credit card bills, and incur interest.

19

You need mechanisms to manage cash flow

Cash flow is tricky. Bills come due at different times. The timing of paychecks doesn't always work out. And costs from month to month can vary widely. You might budget $50 a month for auto repairs, but in all likelihood you will have zero in auto repair expense for six months and then a $350 repair expense pop up in month seven. That's why sticking to your budget isn't quite enough.

You need to have mechanisms set up to give you cash flow buffer every month. Effectively, there are three main things you can do:

- build up a short-term savings account that provides buffer for month-to-month cash flow fluctuations
- use credit cards to defer cash outlay
- set up an overdraft account, or another loan vehicle, to use when you become cash flow negative

A short-term savings account makes for a great cash flow buffer, however you need to make sure you have the discipline to contribute to the account when you are cash flow positive so that you don't erode from your savings in months when you are cash flow negative. Using a short-term savings account has the additional benefit of serving double-duty as your emergency fund.

Used appropriately, credit cards provide a couple of powerful financial benefits. One, the right card provides benefits back to you when you use it in terms of cash back or points. Second, and perhaps more importantly, it allows you to pay for things up to 30 days later than you would have to pay for it if you paid by cash or directly out of your checking account. Some corporate cards have an even longer grace period (i.e. 60 days). With a little bit of thought, you can use these grace periods to even out your cash flow.

As a final safety net, setting up an overdraft account at your bank, or a different variable line-of-credit, will give you a source of cash to pull from when you are cash flow negative. The downside of this solution is that the cost of the buffer is higher in terms of overdraft fees and/or interest charges. The upside is that it can be set up to automatically cover a negative balance in your account, in case you don't notice that you've gone cash flow negative.

In summary, make sure you have mechanisms in place for managing your cash flow.

20

Cash flow issues are not necessarily budget issues

A common misconception is that a negative balance in your checking account indicates overspending in the budget. Certainly, this can happen. However, it's important to recognize whether the issue is a budget issue (not having enough money) or a cash flow issue (the timing of the money).

Budget issues should be resolved as quickly as possible, because a budget that isn't balanced will continue to erode your assets or grow your debts.

Cash flow issues are more transient. It's ok to have the occasional cash flow issue providing you are still tracking overall to your average monthly budget and you have mechanisms in place to handle the cash flow issues.

The key is being able to recognize the difference.

21

Balancing your checkbook is a waste of time

Once upon a time, we had to balance our checkbook to understand how much money we had in the account and to make sure we didn't end up cash flow negative. We also balanced our checkbook to ensure that the bank didn't make any mistakes as they manually entered transactions captured from hand written checks.

These days are long gone. Your near-real-time account balance can now be accessed at any time from any device via the Internet. Most banking transactions are automated and bank errors are so exceedingly rare that it's hardly worth the time to double-check your statements.

Save yourself the time and energy of balancing your checkbook and instead focus on the bigger financial questions captured elsewhere in this book.

22

Auditing your expenses makes sense

While balancing your checkbook is a waste of time, auditing your expenses every month or so does make sense. The audit should be a sampling, and the intent isn't to reconcile your account but rather to detect fraudulent charges (charges that you didn't make) so that you can contest them and get them removed.

Auditing your expenses also gives you the chance to double-check how you are doing against your budget.

RISK MANAGEMENT: PROTECT FOR THE UNEXPECTED

23

Insurance companies make money

This is how all insurance works. You pay the insurance company small amounts (called premiums) every month or on some other periodic basis, and in exchange the insurance company agrees to pay you a large amount if something bad happens. You can insure basically anything, but the main types of insurance that apply to people like you and I include:

- renter's insurance that reimburses you if your personal property gets stolen or damaged, if you don't own a house

- auto insurance that reimburses you if you get in an accident or if your car gets stolen or damaged

- home insurance that reimburses you if your house or your personal property gets stolen or damaged

- liability insurance, which is often included in the policies above, and that reimburses you if you get sued

- health insurance that reimburses you for expenses related to your health

- dental insurance that reimburses you for dental expenses

- vision insurance that reimburses you for expenses related to vision

- life insurance that pays your family if you die

- disability insurance that reimburses you if you become disabled and can't work

Insurance is a critically important component of your overall financial security. Most of us can't afford to replace our house if it burns down, so we need insurance just in case.

It's important to remember though, that insurance companies make money. In fact, they make a lot of money. What this tells us is that, on average, they take in more small payments overall than they pay out in large payments.

24

Insurance is for catastrophes, not the little stuff

Since insurance companies take in more money than they put out, we can conclude that insurance is not a good financial investment. Indeed, that's not its purpose. It's not an investment; it's a protection. Its purpose is to protect you from financial catastrophe. Unless you have millions of dollars sitting around (in which case, you could consider yourself "self-insured"), you flat out can't afford to rebuild your house, pay hundreds of thousands of dollars in a lawsuit, or pay your bills if you become too sick to work.

You probably can afford to replace your cell phone, cover that small ding in your car, or replace that broken window. Therefore, these are things that you should typically not insure.

That said, there are a handful of other reasons, besides protecting against financial catastrophe, that might lead you to buying insurance:

- some insurance is required by law, at legal minimums. This includes car, health, and home insurance (which is required by your bank if you have a mortgage)

- the insurance might be subsidized by your employer, or otherwise discounted through a group rate such that it's cheaper to pay for the insurance than the cost of services (examples include health, dental, and vision)
- you may be willing to pay for "peace of mind", the knowledge that you could afford to cover a loss, but you don't want to have to worry about it

In general though, you should only buy insurance for financial catastrophes, not for the little stuff.

25

You want the largest deductible you can afford

If there is an event, for which the insurance company should pay you, you file a claim. Part of virtually every claim, is the payment of a deductible. The deductible is effectively your contribution to the claim and it exists to ensure that people aren't filing claims willy-nilly. The deductible effectively sets a threshold for when you engage your insurance company.

For example, if your deductible on your auto policy is $1000, and you have a small fender-bender resulting in $500 in damage, you wouldn't file a claim with your insurance because you'd have to contribute $1000 (your deductible) towards the repair before the insurance company pays a dime.

When you buy an insurance policy, you sometimes get to pick your deductible. Because the insurance company pays out less frequently with higher deductible policies, the cost of those policies are less expensive (i.e. have lower monthly premiums).

Because we know that insurance is not an investment, but a protection against financial catastrophe, that means you should generally pick the largest deductible you can afford.

26

Life insurance is really salary insurance

Remember, insurance is a protection against financial catastrophe. Certainly, if you were to die that would constitute a catastrophe. But what would the financial impact be?

When you have a family to support, the financial impact is absolutely catastrophic, and you need to have enough life insurance to protect your family's financial position when they no longer have your salary to rely upon.

Before you have a family, when no one but you is reliant on your salary, life insurance doesn't make sense. You need your income, but if you pass away you won't be around to spend your lost income anyway.

By the same logic, you should stay away from insurance for your kids. Since they wouldn't be working, they wouldn't have a salary to protect against loss.

27

Comparing insurance policies can save you thousands

Even when insurance is offered through your employer, there will likely be multiple options. In general, insurance policies that have better benefits will have higher monthly premiums. Fortunately, insurance is a financial instrument and it's relatively easy to compare policies on the basis of total cost. At the end of the day, you are trying to minimize how much money you have to spend in total; including premiums, deductibles, and coinsurance.

An insurance premium is the amount of money that you need to spend (usually on a monthly basis) to keep the insurance policy in force. A deductible is the amount that you have to pay out of pocket (either by event or over a period of time, usually a year) before the insurance starts to kick in. And finally, co-insurance is the percentage of each covered expense that you have to cover yourself.

For health, dental, and vision insurance, the economic analysis comes down to estimating how much you are going to need to use the insurance. Then you can calculate how much you will end up spending in total on health, dental, or vision in conjunction with each policy.

Suppose you are comparing two sample health insurance policies (deliberately simplified for this example):

-   The standard plan costs $100/month, and covers 80% of your healthcare costs (i.e. 20% coinsurance) after a $2000 deductible.
-   The preferred plan costs $200/month, and covers 90% of your healthcare costs (i.e. 10% coinsurance) after a $1000 deductible.

If you anticipate spending $4000 on healthcare over the year, the standard plan would cost you $3,600 ($1200 in premiums plus the $2000 deductible plus 20% of the remaining $2000). The preferred plan would cost you $3,700 ($2400 in premiums plus the $1000 deductible plus 10% of the remaining $3000). Go with the standard plan.

However, if you anticipate spending $8000 on healthcare over the year (and healthcare is expensive!), the standard plan would cost you $4,400 ($1200 in premiums plus the $2000 deductible plus 20% of the remaining $6000). The preferred plan would cost you $4,100 ($2400 in premiums plus $1000 in deductible plus 10% of the remaining $7000). Go with the preferred plan.

You may not know what to expect in healthcare costs for the year. In general, if you don't know what to expect and you are young and healthy, seek to minimize your healthcare premiums.

For other insurance policies, it's even easier. For these policies, you just need to estimate the minimum amount of insurance you need and then pick the policy that provides you that amount of coverage for the lowest premiums. Just make sure that from a coverage perspective, the policies are comparable.

28

Extended warranties are for suckers

Whenever you make a medium to large purchase, especially on electronics, the salesperson will try and sell you an extended warranty or protection plan. The reason why they try and sell these warranties is because they are extremely profitable; often the store makes more money on the warranty than on the product itself.

An extended warranty is just another form of an insurance policy, and insurance companies make a lot of money by bringing in more money than they ever pay out.

Therefore, you are generally best off passing on offers for an extended warranty. The only possible exception would be if you had more information than the sales person about the probability of the purchase getting broken. For example, if you are notoriously prone for breaking your cell phone at a rate far above the average rate that the insurance company uses to set the price of the warranty, it could potentially be worthwhile to purchase the warranty. You would need to make sure you understand clearly the limitations and benefits of the policy to make sure your covered; and in any case this would be a very exceptional case for purchasing the extended warranty.

In general, they are a bad deal.

29

Fraud happens

Billions of financial transactions are made every day, and of course that draws in criminals to attempt to steal money along the way. At multiple points in your life, you will be a victim of fraud or attempted fraud, in terms of charges to your credit card or bank account that were not made by you.

The most important thing for you to know, is that you are <u>not</u> responsible if someone else accesses your money fraudulently. This is a key benefit of using a bank and/or a credit card to pay for things.

To protect yourself from fraud:

- Audit your bank and credit card statements. If you see a charge that you didn't make, call the bank or credit card company immediately.
- Maintain physical control of your bank and credit cards. If you discover that any are missing, or you know you misplaced one, call the bank or credit card company and cancel the card. They will send you a new card right away.
- Be alert when you are using your credit card or your PIN at an ATM. Make sure no one (or no device, like a camera or a suspicious electronic reader) can see or read your card.
- Don't share your PIN with anyone.

- Protect your sensitive personal information, like your social security number; providing it only when required and only with trusted entities (for example, government, educational institutions, etc.).

If someone commits fraud, or attempts to commit fraud:

- The bank or credit card company may call you, either in person or with an automated message, asking you to verify whether you authorized the transaction. Respond right away.
- If the bank doesn't call you, but you notice fraudulent activity, reach out to the bank or credit card company right away to report the issue. If the fraudulent transactions already went through, it might take some time to get the money credited back to your account. Generally speaking, you will get the charges reversed faster with a credit card than if you need to get the money re-deposited back into your account by your bank.
- Review all of your accounts to determine if it's isolated to one card or if it's more widespread through your accounts. If it's widespread, it might be a symptom of identity theft, which is a much bigger deal, and will require police involvement.

30

Anyone can lose their job

Maybe the largest risk to your financial health; given the relative likelihood, consequence, and inability to control many of the risk factors; is losing your job.

There may be a misconception that only people who are bad at their job get fired. Certainly people who are not good at their job do get fired; but far more people lose their job for other reasons, not related to their performance.

For example:

-   Companies restructure and whole departments go away.
-   Companies merge with one another, creating redundancies that mean someone is no longer needed.
-   Companies cut back the number of employees across the board because their business outlook drops.
-   Individuals that get hired into new leadership positions routinely swap out their old reports for people that they bring in from the outside and know and trust.
-   Whole companies, even very large ones, go bankrupt or disappear seemingly overnight (e.g. Enron, Arthur Andersen, Blockbuster, Borders, etc.)

The important thing is to recognize that this risk exists in a very real way for all employees. Later in this book, we will discuss some strategies to help mitigate it.

SAVINGS: CONVERTING INCOME TO ASSETS

31

Compound interest is magical

"Compound interest is the eighth wonder of the world. He who understands it, earns it ... he who doesn't ... pays it."

-   Albert Einstein

Compound interest is a financial concept where any interest that is earned in an investment is added back into the principal to earn interest on itself. This results in interest being paid on interest, and that interest earning interest, and so on and so on.

One hundred dollars left in your checking account will still be one hundred dollars in thirty years. In thirty years, that same one hundred dollars moved to your savings account becomes about $150.00. In the stock market that same hundred dollars turns into almost $500.00. You didn't do anything more than change where you put the money, but the outcome is very different. That's the magic of compound interest.

There is a cool shortcut to estimating the impact of compound interest. If you divide the number 70 by the estimated annual rate of return you can approximate the number of years it would take for your money to double. For example, at a 10% annual growth rate, your money would double every 7 years (70 divided by 10).

Leverage the magic of compound interest everywhere you can by making sure your free cash ends up converted to an asset with a return (or a liability where compound interest is working against you).

In summary, compound interest is magical.

32

Saving for retirement starts now

The day you start your new job, make sure you contribute the maximum allowed to your retirement account (i.e. 401(k) or 403(b)).

Here's why:

- It's easiest to save the money you never see. Since you never had the money, you won't miss it.
- You have less expenses right now than you will have during the rest of your lifetime.
- Your contributions are tax deferred (or in the case of a Roth, the earnings are tax exempt). This is free money courtesy of the US government, for being so fiscally responsible as to save for your own retirement. For example, because of the tax advantage, contributing $1000 to a standard 401(k) only reduces your take home pay by about $600.00. Free money!
- Compound interest is magical. The longer the money sits in your retirement account, the faster and bigger it grows. $15,000 contributed to your retirement account at 23, could be worth about a million dollars when you retire at age 62! By contrast, if you wait until you are 30

(only 7 years later), that same $15,000 will only be worth about $500,000 at retirement.[2]

- The sooner you start contributing, the more time you have to contribute. In addition to the magic of compound interest, the sooner you start contributing the more you can contribute over your lifetime, since the government caps your annual contribution.

In the United States, in most cases you will be required to pay Social Security Taxes. Don't mistake this for adequate retirement savings! While Social Security does provide retirement benefits (as well as disability benefits) once you've worked long enough, it's not nearly enough to live on. Therefore you need to start right away to generate your own retirement nest egg.

---

[2] This math assumes an aggressive investment strategy of investing 100% in the stock market, which over the last century or so has historically returned about 11% per year.

33

You need short-term savings

You need to have a savings account set up for short-term needs, like as a cash-flow buffer or when an unexpected expense temporarily upsets your budget. This short-term account needs to be low risk (which means it will have a low return), and highly liquid. A savings account at your bank works fine. A few thousand dollars is sufficient.

Since undoubtedly you will also have some things that you want to save up for, like a vacation, a car, or Christmas shopping; this is a place where you can kill two birds with one stone. Set up a savings account (or multiple savings accounts) and contribute to it (them) on a consistent basis over a period of time, and you will have the money you need for your big purchase, all the while having the short-term buffer account you need. And since you are probably always going to be saving for something, it's very easy to set up an automatic transfer from your checking account to the savings account(s) to help you stay disciplined.

34

You need an emergency nest egg account

You need an emergency nest egg account with at least three months of salary saved in a low risk, highly liquid account.

This account isn't for covering short-term cash flow issues, nor is it for saving up for a big purchase. This account is effectively self-funded insurance against a financial catastrophe that insurance companies don't insure you against; losing your job.

If you lose your job, in all likelihood you'll receive some severance (an additional payment at the time of your termination) that is meant to help bridge your finances until you find your next job. But you can't count on that severance being there or being sufficient. Losing your salary would indeed be a financially catastrophic event. Therefore, you need to have some financial protection against the real risk of losing your job.

35

College savings starts at birth

Just as retirement savings should start the day you birth your career, college savings should start the day you birth your child. The reasons are exceedingly similar:

- The government provides attractive tax advantages for saving for college. There are multiple investment vehicles, but the most common one is called a 529 plan. In a 529 plan, the earnings are tax free (as long as you use the money for college). On top of that, many states make some portion of the contribution tax deductible. Free money!

- Compound interest is magical. The longer the money sits in your college savings account, the faster and bigger it grows. $12,000 contributed to the account the first year, could be worth about $50,000 when your child leaves for college! By contrast, if you wait until they are 5, that same $12,000 will only be worth about $34,000 when they leave for school.[3]

---

[3] This math assumes a moderately aggressive investment strategy yielding a return of 8% per year. Because there is a shorter timeframe for college savings than for retirement savings, we are more sensitive to risk, so we need to be a bit more conservative in the assumptions.

- Your child will be listed as the beneficiary of the savings account, but you will still be the official owner. This means that it will have less negative impact on calculating financial aid for college.
- In the event that your child doesn't go to college or gets a scholarship to pay for it, you don't lose the money or the tax advantage. You can simply change the beneficiary to your next child, use it for graduate school, or withdraw it for other purposes (limitations apply).

Start saving early!

36

Retirement savings takes priority over all others

If you are simultaneously saving for a whole bunch of different purposes, how do you prioritize your efforts?

Experts agree that you should prioritize your retirement savings over all others. The amount you can contribute to retirement, while still receiving the tax benefits is capped, so said another way, you should always be capping out your retirement contributions before saving for anything else.

Here's why:

- In general, the tax advantages on retirement are better than on other investments.
- Because you are long way from retiring, that maximizes the amount of time that your money can grow.
- Because you are a long way from retiring, you aren't as sensitive to risk in the investment. You don't care if your return goes up or down year over year. On average, that smooths out over a long timeframe.
- If you are contributing consistently over a long time frame, you have the additional advantage of "dollar-cost averaging" your investment which further reduces the

risk. In other words, if you are contributing the same amount of money every month to retirement, and the stock market plummets; guess what, you are now buying more stock at a steep, steep discount! This ends up tempering the impact that the plummet has on the existing stock you already own.

- Retirement assets are generally excluded from calculating financial aid for college.
- If you do ever get in a bind and need to access your retirement funds early, there are mechanisms to do so (for example, 401(k) loans). However, you want to be very careful with this option because it erodes the other advantages that we've just outlined.

In summary, always prioritize saving for retirement.

INVESTING: MAKING YOUR MONEY WORK

37

There are many different types of investments

There is a virtually unlimited number of different investment vehicles, including investments that package up other investments made up of investments of investments. Financial gurus and investment brokers continue to invent new ways to make (or take) money all the time. That said, here is a short list of investment vehicles you are likely to come across and need to know about:

- Lending Vehicles
    - o Savings Accounts
    - o Money Market Accounts
    - o Certificates of Deposit
    - o Bonds

- Ownership Vehicles
    - o Stocks
    - o Mutual Funds
    - o Real Estate
    - o Commodities and Collectibles

38

Lending vehicles tend to be low risk and liquid

We call these investments "lending vehicles" because what is actually happening is that you are loaning your hard earned cash to another party in exchange for them paying you interest:

- Savings Accounts
- Money Market Accounts
- Certificates of Deposit
- Bonds

It may be strange to think of a savings account as a lending vehicle, but the reason why the bank is paying you interest is so that they can use your money for other investments (like loaning the money to other customers in the form of auto or home loans). Savings accounts are guaranteed by the government (via the Federal Deposit Insurance Corporation, or FDIC) which makes them extremely low risk. As long as the United States exists, your money will be safe. Because it's so low risk, the returns tend to be very low.

Money Market accounts are effectively the same as a savings account, but instead of opening it with your bank, you open it with a brokerage or mutual fund company. Money Market accounts tend to pay a better rate than a savings account even though they play the same exact function.

Certificates of Deposit (CDs) pay a higher interest rate than a savings or money market account, but the tradeoff is in liquidity. When you open a CD, you "lock up" your money for a certain period of time that you can't access it. In other words, you are committing your money to the bank for a period of time that could range from one month to five years, in exchange for a better interest rate. In general, the longer the lockup, the better the rate.

Bonds are more complicated. Bonds are loans to governments or corporations. They vary widely in return and risk. Some bonds also have tax advantages. What's interesting about bonds is that they are easily traded on the securities exchange similar to stocks. So in addition to providing a return, they also have a value in the market in which you can buy or sell them. In that sense, they have the characteristics of both a lending vehicle and an ownership vehicle. You can make money through the return on the bond or you can make money by selling the bond for more than you bought it for.

Lending vehicles, due to their low risk and high liquidity, should be an important part of your financial plan.

39

Ownership vehicles create wealth

Wealthy individuals generally get wealthy through ownership vehicles. They invest in stocks, real estate, and/or small businesses. Ownership vehicles have higher risk and higher return than lending vehicles, but they are the key to financial independence. The four types of ownership vehicles you are most likely to have in your portfolio are:

- Stocks
- Mutual Funds
- Real Estate
- Commodities and Collectibles

Stocks are the most common investment vehicle. Stocks represent an ownership share in a publically owned company. If you buy 100 shares of Apple stock, and Apple has issued one billion shares, you would literally own 0.00001% of the Apple Corporation (one billion divided by 100). This would mean you would receive that percentage of their overall quarterly earnings, and you would have that percentage of a vote at annual shareholder meetings (if you cared enough to go to the meeting and vote, but few people do).

More important than earnings or voting rights, is the fact that stocks can be bought and sold on the securities exchange. Wealth is created when stocks are sold for more than the buyer originally paid for them. Due to factors like inflation, growing interest in stocks, and overall global economic growth, the stock market has returned an average of about 11% a year over the past century.

The downside of stocks is risk. While the stock market has grown consistently over a long time frame, over short time frames it is extremely volatile. It can drop or climb precipitously in a single day or slowly drop or climb over the course of a decade.

Mutual Funds are designed to help mitigate the risk of buying individual stocks. Mutual Funds are collections of stocks in different companies, managed by a professional money manager. It mitigates some of the inherent risk in buying stocks through a concept called diversification. The concept is that the chance of one stock dropping is very high, but the chances of multiple stocks dropping simultaneously is lower. Mutual funds diversify not with just individual companies, but with whole industries, geographies, company sizes, etc. That diversification coupled with professional money managers makes investment in mutual funds less risky than investing in individual stocks.

Real Estate refers to the purchase of property like your home, rental property, land, etc. Real Estate, like the stock market, is vulnerable to short-term value fluctuations, but in the long-term has delivered good historical returns. Real Estate has some other unique advantages including a finite supply, the ability to use it to live in or generate income from renters, the ability to leverage borrowed money, and the benefit of real estate friendly tax law.

Commodities and collectibles are ownership vehicles of a

different flavor altogether. Commodities like precious metals and collectibles like comic books and baseball cards are not likely to generate wealth by themselves, but they are generally low risk (due to the fact that supply is limited) and their value tends to be inversely proportional to non-physical investments like stocks. In other words, investors tend to gravitate to low risk investments like silver and gold when the stock market looks shaky.

The important thing to remember is that ownership vehicles are the key to building wealth.

40

You should take advantage of company stock

If you work for a public company you may have access to stock for free or at a discount. Even if you work for a private company, some private companies offer "shares" of the company via what is effectively a promise of stock or profit share when the company is sold. Taking advantage of these company perks can dramatically accelerate your wealth creation.

In a public company there are a few different mechanisms for employees to receive stock:

- A stock grant is a grant of "free" stock from the company to the employee. The grant is usually associated with an annual bonus for performance or as a celebratory grant upon promotion or reaching a career milestone.

- A stock option grant is a grant of stock at a fixed price (called the strike price). It grants the employee the right to buy a set amount of stock at a later date at the strike price, which is generally lower than the price you'd normally pay down the road.

- An Employee Stock Purchase Plan (ESPP) is a program that allows employees to buy stock at a discount from the price available in the open market. It's optional, but generally available to all employees. If your company offers an ESPP, you should purchase as much discounted stock as they allow. Free Money!

It's in your best interest to take full advantage of these company perks, but there are two "watch outs":

- You need to make sure that you don't end up with too much of your portfolio tied up in your company stock. Imagine being an Enron employee with millions of dollars in Enron stock the day the company disappeared. It happened. Several hundred employees simultaneously lost their life savings <u>and</u> their salary. This issue is easy to mitigate by proactively and periodically selling a portion of your company stock and re-investing the profits in other investment vehicles.

- "Free Money" is not really free. The government still taxes it, and the taxes on these instruments can be a bit complicated. The government will tax your stock earnings, which effectively is the difference between what you sell the stock for, and how much you personally paid for the stock (called your cost basis). In a stock grant, your cost basis is zero; for stock options, your cost basis is your strike price; and for an ESPP, your cost basis is what you paid for the stock. What complicates it, is that the government taxes these transactions at different times (for example, the difference between the value of the shares on the day you receive the shares and your cost basis will generally get taxed when you receive the shares and your earnings off of that cost basis will be taxed when you sell the shares).

Watch outs aside, taking advantage of the company perks around stock ownership is an excellent way to build wealth.

41

Professionals should handle the important stuff

In your portfolio of assets, you will have some large accounts (e.g. your retirement account) and some smaller accounts (e.g. other savings or investment accounts).

In general, you should leave the big stuff to the professional money managers. These folks spend every waking minute of every day paying attention to what's going on in the market and determining the best way to maximize return while minimizing risk. You have your own job, and you don't have the same time or focus to spend on the markets. This means you should leverage mutual funds for your large investment accounts.

Of course, there's no harm is self-managing the smaller accounts as you learn how to invest (and in particular, how to diversify). Just recognize that learning to invest can be costly; you're certain to make some mistakes along the way and suffer some losses. Consider it the cost of education.

42

Diversification is the most important investment strategy

After compound interest, diversification might be the next most magical concept in personal finance. Every investment has a return and a risk, but packaging investments together in a portfolio can significantly reduce the risk while less significantly impacting the return.

The reason why diversification works is because it is less likely that multiple investments, companies, geographies, etc. will crash at the same time, making for a smoother overall return on the portfolio as a whole. In fact, some investments tend to react to each other in opposite ways, which makes the combination of them essentially self-leveling. For example, bond values tend to go up when stock values go down (in general, but not always).

Diversification can be beneficial in almost every dimension you can think of:

- Investment
- Investment Type
- Industry
- Size
- Geography

- Money manager
- Brokerage
- Tax treatment
- Customer base
- Etc.

As you think about your financial portfolio, always think in terms of diversification. It lowers your risk and gives you peace of mind, knowing that you aren't as exposed to the whims of the financial markets.

43

Longer timeframes warrant more aggressive investments

In essence, risk is a measure of an investment's "volatility" (its tendency to have its return go up or down suddenly). If you have a long timeframe until you are going to use the money, you can afford to incur more risk. Furthermore, since return tends to be correlated with risk; you want higher returns and higher risk in investments with a longer timeframe.

Consider this example. If your retirement account is going to be around for 40 years until you even start to draw money out of it, do you care if the value in the account drops 50% every 10 years, but subsequently recovers? What really matters is the value of the account at the end of 40 years. Of course, as you get closer to retirement your timeframe gets shorter, so you'll make adjustments to the investment to lower your risk profile (and subsequently your returns). So you want to maximize your returns now, while you have plenty of time.

Longer timeframes give you room to incur greater risk.

44

Panic and exuberance lead to bad decisions

Investing requires discipline, and emotion is the enemy of discipline. In terms of investment in ownership vehicles, the goal is always to buy at a low price and sell it at a high price. While obvious, it's very easy to lose sight of this when markets get volatile.

When the markets drop quickly, many people panic and sell off their investments. This the absolute worst response to their investments dropping; they are selling low. Stocks being cheap are the time to buy, not the time to sell.

Similarly, when the market, or even a particular stock, is hot (the price is rising quickly) many people get caught up in the exuberant atmosphere and rush to buy in. They are buying high. Stocks being expensive are not the time to buy.

Of course, determining whether an investment is cheap or expensive at a point in time, is easier said than done. This is the same reason that day trading as a hobby is a bad idea. Day trading (frequent buying and selling) is attempting to time the market based on superficial data about the price and value of an investment. It's more akin to gambling than investing. It's important to be a disciplined investor, with a long term view, who avoids making decisions based on emotion.

CREDIT CARDS: FRIEND AND FOE

45

It's important to understand how credit cards work

Understanding how credit card companies make money is important, because it allows you to maximize your return from your credit card while minimizing how much money you spend on their services.

Done correctly, you can and should use your credit cards as much as you want, reap the rewards and benefits, and pay <u>nothing</u>.

Credit cards make money in four main ways:

- They collect fees from us as users of the card. These fees differ by card and include annual fees, over-the-limit fees, late fees, cash-advance fees, etc.
- They collect interest from us on any outstanding balance that gets carried over from month to month.
- They get a cut of each purchase (1-4% depending on the card and purchase), paid for by the vendor.
- They sell our name and contact information to other companies so that those companies can try and sell us other stuff (via junk mail, cold calling, etc.).

The first two ways they make money come directly out of our pocket while the last two payment streams are paid by someone else.

Knowing this is important, as it will allow you to minimize what you pay for using your credit cards.

46

Avoiding credit card fees and interest charges is critical

Credit card companies collectively make hundreds of billions of dollars a year. They are astute for-profit companies that are focused on making money. That means that they actively push to increase the revenue from both the fees and the interest that they collect from us.

Annual fees are fees that you pay the credit card company every year for the card. In some cases, annual fees are fine because the benefit of using the card (i.e. the rewards program or exclusive services) outweighs the annual fee. That said, there are plenty of cards out there without an annual fee, so only sign up for an annual fee if you know it's worth it.

All of the other fees that the credit card charges are effectively "screw up" fees. In other words, it's money you pay to the credit card company when you "screw up." Forget to pay the bill on time? Cha-ching! Run over your credit limit? Cha-ching! Decide to pull cash out off your credit card, as opposed to your checking or savings account? Cha-ching! It's in your best interest to avoid these fees.

The even bigger cut to the credit card companies is actually the interest on outstanding balances. Credit card companies encourage you to carry a balance on their card every month. Of course they do, since the interest rate you pay them is typically significantly higher than if you obtained the cash some other way, like through a traditional loan (or better yet, from your own income or assets).

If you find yourself in a place where you do have a credit card balance that you can't pay off, manage it as a debt within your asset and debt portfolio. Consider the negative return on the debt with respect to all of your other debts and assets, and make decisions that benefit your overall financial situation.

In summary, if you pay off your balance on time every month, you will not be charged any interest or fees. Automatic payments can help with this. If you set up your credit card payment to be automatically paid-in-full out of your checking account every month, you're guaranteed to not be paying credit card interest or "screw-up" fees.

47

Maximizing credit card benefits is smart

Remember that credit card companies don't just make their money off of their card members. They also take a sizeable cut (1-4%) of every purchase, which is paid by the store that sold you the goods. Credit card companies want you to buy a lot of stuff with their card, even if you do pay it off in full every month.

This works to our advantage, because it makes the credit card companies compete for us to use their card; typically in the form of benefits and rewards.

There are thousands of different cards out there, each with its own set of benefits and rewards. Benefits could include things like exclusive access to concerts or airport lounges, travel insurance, or purchase protection. Rewards typically come in two flavors: cash-back, or points that can be used for merchandise, travel, etc. And of course, all credit cards have some benefits inherent to them like the convenience of not having to carry cash, the ability to defer your cash outlay 30 days, etc.

It's smart to understand the benefits and rewards with your credit cards and to maximize your return from these powerful tools. It's also smart to periodically shop for better benefits and rewards, and change credit cards as appropriate.

TAXES:
UNCLE SAM'S
PIECE OF THE PIE

48

It's important to understand how income taxes work

You don't have to be a tax expert, but you do need to have some idea how income taxes work. In summary, they work like this:

- The government estimates your tax liability and withdraws estimated taxes from every paycheck.
- By around April 15th every year, you need to file tax documentation for the previous calendar year.
- That tax documentation is used to calculate the amount of tax you actually owed for the previous year.
- If you paid more in estimated taxes than what you actually owed, you get a refund. If you paid less than what you owed, you have to send them a check for the difference.

Of course, this is a gross simplification of what's really involved. But the basics are important. Other things you need to know:

- There are several different taxes that come out of your paycheck, including Federal Income Tax, State Income Tax, Local Income Tax, and Social Security Tax.

- Your estimated taxes that the government withdraws from your paycheck are based on your answers to the W-4 form you fill out with your employer.
- If the estimated taxes that come out of your paycheck are much too low, not only will you owe the government a lot of money in April, but they may also charge you interest and fees on top of what you owe.
- Calculating the taxes you owe when you file every April 15th is complicated due to the fact that the tax law is complicated and the government gives you credits and deductions for certain expenses. For example, depending on how you file, you can receive a tax deduction for mortgage interest and/or contributions to charity.
- In general, the more money you make, the more you pay in taxes. That's due to two factors. First, taxes are calculated as a percentage of your income (after certain adjustments calculated when you file), so the same percentage of a higher income means higher taxes. Second, the tax rate percentage itself increases as your income moves through different tax brackets. In other words, your first $10,000 of income might be taxed at a 10% rate, but your income from $10,001 to $40,000 might be taxed at a 15% rate (numbers are illustrative, the brackets and rates change periodically).
- Income Taxes are just one type of tax that the government uses to raise money from private citizens. Other taxes include sales tax, property tax, and use tax. These taxes don't come out of your paycheck; they are paid when you make taxable purchases, on a separate periodic payment schedule, or when you use taxable products or services.

49

Your W-4 is important

The government estimates your tax liability based on a document you fill out with your employer called a W-4. This is what determines how much gets taken out of each paycheck, which subsequently determines the following April whether you get a refund or have to write a check to the IRS.

It's important that your W-4 be as accurate as possible, otherwise one of two things could happen:

- Not enough tax will be taken from each paycheck, resulting in you having a tax payment due in April. If you're not planning on making a large tax payment, it could be very disruptive to your finances. On top of that, if the payment due is large enough, the government will tack on fees and interest.

- Too much tax will be taken from each paycheck, resulting in you getting money back in April. While it might sound nice to get a large tax refund, from a financial perspective it's not a great way to save money. The government doesn't pay you any interest on the money you overpaid them over the course of the year; you are better off paying your taxes accurately out of your paychecks and investing the extra money.

You can update your W-4 with your employer at any time. You should update it each year after you file your taxes, if you find that you are getting too big a return, or paying too large a payment. You should also update it after large life events or if you have any unexpected untaxed windfalls.

50

Tax considerations matter

The tax treatment of debts and investments can vary widely and materially. Examples are below. This is not a comprehensive list, and a myriad of rules, limitations, and caveats apply:

- Mortgage interest is typically tax deductible.
- Contributions to a traditional retirement account is typically tax deductible.
- Earnings from a Roth IRA or 529 College Savings Account are typically tax deductible.
- Spending on child care and education is subject to certain tax credits.

Tax law changes every year, but the important thing to remember is that you need to consider the tax implications as you make financial decisions.

51

Contributing to a healthcare FSA is free money

Many employers offer their employees the opportunity to contribute money pre-tax out of their paycheck to a healthcare Flexible Spending Account (FSA). The government legislates how these accounts work:

- You can contribute money to the FSA, up to a defined contribution limit.
- You can use the money in the FSA to pay for qualified medical, dental, and vision expenses.
- Any money you have left over in the account at the end of the year is forfeited.

Since you can use an FSA to pay for medical expenses tax free, it's a great way to save significant money. You just need to ensure that your medical expenses use up all of your contributions; otherwise, you end up forfeiting some of your hard-earned money. The definition of a qualified expense is fairly liberal, so it's not hard to make sure you use up any remaining account balance late in the year by stocking up on contacts, glasses, prescription medications, etc.

52

It's worthwhile to know how to file

Again, you don't need to be a tax expert, but you should have a basic idea on how to file your taxes, even if you leave the heavy lifting to a tax professional.

The main tax form is called the 1040. There are simplified versions of this form (called the 1040EZ and the 1040A) that are available if you are below a certain salary and your tax requirements are simple. Otherwise, you will file the full 1040.

There are several supplements to the 1040 that are used for specific tax scenarios. Common examples include (not comprehensive):

- Schedule A, used for itemized deductions
- Schedule B, used to report interest and stock dividends
- Schedule D, used to report gains and losses from stocks

There are really only two options for filing your taxes: you can file them yourself, or you can hire a professional. Especially early in your professional life, you can do your taxes yourself because your financial situation won't be very complicated. Doing your taxes yourself means using tax software, like TurboTax, which walks you through a questionnaire and populates and files the appropriate forms on your behalf.

BUYING VS RENTING: THE TRADEOFFS

53

Many things can be bought or rented

You probably don't think about it very much, but often you have a financial choice as to whether to buy a product or rent/lease it. Many products are both purchasable and rentable, including some things you don't normally think of:

- Houses, Condos, and Apartments
- Cars
- Trucks
- Tools
- Mobile Phones
- Electronics
- Moving Supplies
- Catering and Party Supplies
- Furniture
- Bicycles
- Sporting Equipment

54

In general, buying is better in the long term

Generally speaking, it's financially better in the long term to buy rather than rent. When a company or an individual is renting a product, they set the price so that the total income they make from renting the product multiple times covers the purchase cost and provides them a profit. So, buying normally makes sense over renting.

55

Renting has its place

While buying is generally better in the long term, there are specific cases when renting/leasing has its place. For example:

- Limited Use – If you are aren't likely to use the product more than once, or if you are only ever going to use the product for a short period of time, renting may make sense.

- Convenience – If you are traveling for example, you may not want to bring your golf clubs; you may just want to rent when you get there.

- Storage – If you don't have the room to keep a bunch of excess party supplies in storage, it might be easier to just rent them when you need them, and then return them to the rental facility.

- Desire for New and Shiny (Cars) – In the case of cars, leasing may make sense if you want to get a new car every few years. You pay more in the long run leasing rather than owning and driving the same car for a longer period of time, but it's also about what you value as an individual. The "Desire for New and Shiny" rationale could also apply for other things like electronics, if for example, you wanted to rent your smartphone and upgrade to the newest model as soon as it was released.

- High Switching Costs (Housing) – In the case of housing, because there are significant costs in the purchase and selling process (closing costs, financing costs, realtor costs, etc.), if you aren't going to be living in the same place for at least five years, you may be better off renting a place, instead of buying it.

In these cases, renting has its place.

OUTSOURCING: TIME IS MONEY

56

Time has value

It could be argued that time is our most valuable natural resource. No matter what, you can't ever create more time. So time has value; but the challenge is how to value it.

The easiest way to value time is to think about it in terms of opportunity cost. For example, if you make $50/hour at your job and are missing out on an opportunity to work because you are doing something else, a short-cut would be to say your time is worth $50/hour. Of course, to say that your time is worth your hourly salary is just a crude shortcut. If you are a stay-at-home parent with no salary per se, that certainly doesn't mean that your time has no value. In fact, as a stay-at-home parent, time might be even more scarce which means even more valuable.

If you can put a value on your time, outsourcing decisions become pretty straight forward. If you can go net $50/hour at work while you are paying a lawn service $25/hour to mow your lawn, you should probably take that deal.

Even if you can't put a price tag on your time, the important thing to keep in mind is that <u>time has real material value</u>. Therefore, not everything you can do is worth spending your time on.

57

Sometimes, someone else can do it cheaper

Believe it or not, there are some services that someone else can do cheaper, even if you don't value the time itself. Here is why:

- Special Tools – Some jobs require special tools and the cost to go out and purchase or rent the tools exceed the cost of paying someone who already has the tools to do it.

- Special Skills – Some jobs require special skills that you may not have. So the job may take you four times longer and twice as much material as it takes an expert. If you are looking at the activity as an educational exercise, you might want to do it anyway, but from a financial perspective you are better off letting the expert do it.

- Risk – If you don't know how to build a house, you shouldn't build a house. If you aren't a lawyer (and even if you are), you shouldn't represent yourself in court. Aside from the obvious safety implications, financially you are more likely to incur additional costs down the road when your work falls apart, and that will likely exceed the costs to do it right in the first place.

CAREER

You're most likely going to spend the next 40+ years of your life working (sorry). You'll learn a massive amount over the next several decades, but here are some important things to know to get you off on the right foot.

THE WORK: DOING IT RIGHT

58

Your job is brought to you by your customers

It's been said many different ways and it's a mantra that's as old as business. The customer is always right. Customer is king. Be customer-centric, customer-focused. It's a great philosophy; but it's easy to forget in the day-to-day pressures of business. For my first job out of college, on every paycheck I received was printed the words "brought to you by your clients." I felt like it was a great reminder.

Being customer-centric is more than just a philosophy; there is a very tangible and tactical application of this concept:

<u>Always do what's best for your customer, and everything else will work out.</u>

If you're working directly with customers/clients, this means:

- Prioritize your customer's personal needs ahead of your own. The customer should be listed first in presentations, should have the best seats in the conference room, should be the first to get their food, etc.
- Make your client look good. You don't need to excessively promote yourself or your work. If you make the client look good to her bosses, you will share in her

success and good things will happen for you and your company.

- When in doubt, do what's best for your customer. There will often be times when your customer's interest are in direct conflict with your interest. It might be a need to cut the price, or to add in additional scope or services. In these cases, do what's best for your customer, as it's likely to be a good investment in the long-run. That said, there are two very important caveats:

  o Never compromise on your integrity. Doing something for a customer that feels dirty or unethical is never appropriate, and certain to backfire.

  o Play within reasonable constraints. Doing what's best for the customer doesn't mean giving away the farm. If you have a customer who is unreasonable in taking advantage of your customer/vendor relationship, enabling that behavior is not what's in the best interest of your customer. You will have customers like this. In this scenario, your goal is to train the customer to play fair. If you are unable to get to a place where the customer will be a fair business partner, it's time to resign the customer (stop working with them). Not all customers are good customers.

In summary, always remember that your job is brought to you by your customers.

59

Quality is king

The cornerstone of your professional life, especially early in your career, is doing quality work. If you can't do quality work, little else matters.

Quality work means work that:

- you're proud of
- is accurate in the details (spreadsheets that tie, documents without spelling errors, etc.)
- looks good (well formatted, visually appealing, prints correctly, etc.)

Quality is king.

60

Time is finite

For most of your professional life, you will have more to do than your time allows. Hence, your time will become your professional bottleneck.

Arguably the most important business tool you have at your disposal is your calendar. Make sure you manage your calendar to allow time for your meetings and for all of the things you need to get done.

After your calendar, your to-do list is critically important. There are many apps that can help with this (including Microsoft Outlook Tasks). An effective system for managing your to-dos:

- includes all of your to-dos. You don't want multiple lists.
- includes, at a minimum, the description of the to-do, priority, category (ie. personal vs client related vs internal, etc.), and due date.
- allows you to track your own to-dos as well as follow-ups to check on other people's to-dos.

Be diligent about managing your time so that you can make sure you get done what you need to get done, when it needs to be done.

61

Importance and urgency are different

"What is important is seldom urgent and what is urgent is seldom important."

- Dwight D. Eisenhower

Important tasks contribute to your overall goals, while urgent tasks require immediate attention. These are two different things. They are two different dimensions of a task altogether.

There is a natural tendency to work on tasks that are urgent because they create a lot of noise and anxiety. However, every minute spent on an urgent, but not important task, is an hour that's not spent working on what is important.

In general, you want to work on tasks according to this priority:

- Important and Urgent
- Important but Not Urgent
- Urgent but Not Important
- Not Urgent and Not Important

In summary, avoid the natural tendency to reactively respond to urgent tasks. Instead, work to proactively manage important tasks.

62

Focus is everything

"Things which matter most must never be at the mercy of things which matter least."

-   Johann Wolfgang von Goethe

Time is finite. In addition, most of the time you will already be working at maximum capacity when something else pops onto your plate. Therefore, you will need to be constantly making decisions around prioritization and where to apply your focus.

Since focus dictates how you are spending your most valuable resource, time, it can be argued that it is the single most important work-related tip in this book. Indeed, the most successful people in history will often attribute their unwavering focus on their overall goal as the primary driver of their success.

There are a few things that make focus challenging:

-   You must understand what is important.
-   You must be disciplined enough to deflect or ignore that which is not important.
-   You must be able to articulate what is important, what is not important, and why.

You can't just manage your time. You also have to manage your focus.

63

All things are not equally important

This one seems very obvious. However, most of the time we don't actually treat our activities as though they differ in importance. Consider these every day examples:

- If success on your project depends on intra-team collaboration, how does your time spent working alone on spreadsheets contribute to that success?
- If success at work depends on getting specific deliverables completed, how does your time spent sitting in meetings support that objective?
- If it's important that your customer feels valued, how does your time spent away from your customer help create that perception of value?
- If it's important to you that you get to participate in the everyday moments with your kids and family, how does your travel schedule support that need?
- If your life goal is to be a chef, how does your time spent working in an unrelated field apply to that goal?

Clearly, some things are more important than others; and that relative importance varies in the eyes of the beholder. The important thing is to acknowledge that all things are not created equal.

64

It's important to always keep the end in mind

At the end of the day, success at work is measured in terms of outcomes and deliverables. The process you go through on your way to the outcome is a side effect, not the main purpose.

Given that, it makes sense to always keep in mind what your final deliverable or outcome is, in order that you keep focus on what matters. It's easy to get distracted along the way.

The easiest way to keep the end in mind is to actually draft the final deliverable at the very beginning of the endeavor. The draft might just be a template or an outline or a storyboard, but by iterating on the final deliverable from the beginning, you'll be certain to stay focused on the end, throughout the process.

65

The Pareto Principle is applicable most of the time

The Pareto Principle is named after economist Vilfredo Pareto who observed that 80% of effects tend to come from 20% of the causes. You may be familiar with this principle by its other name: the 80/20 rule.

The 80/20 rule is scarily applicable to almost anything you can think of:

- In economics, 80% of the world's wealth belongs to roughly 20% of the world's population.
- In business, 80% of a company's profits typically come from about 20% of its customers. Also, 80% of a company's complaints come from around 20% of its customers, and 80% of a company's sales come from approximately 20% of its products.
- In software development, 80% of bugs originate from about 20% of the code.
- In project management, 80% of the "noise" comes from 20% of the issues.

Understanding the Pareto Principle and applying it to how you approach work and life is incredibly powerful. Imagine only needing to focus on getting 20% of a project right to get to 80% of project success. Would it change how you approached the project and where you applied your energy? Would you treat all the areas of the project the same, or would you focus on the most important 20%?

66

It's good to under-promise and over-deliver

Especially early in your career, your reputation will center around your ability to get things done and deliver on your promises. Your promises, or commitments, will be made to bosses, colleagues, and even subordinates and will mostly center around what you're going to do and when you are going to have it done by.

You should make it a habit to under-promise, meaning provide a date that is later than when you believe you'll actually have it done; and over-deliver, meaning having your work done ahead of the date you committed to.

This is the best way to establish your reputation as the person who delivers on-time, every time.

67

It only takes one missed commitment to destroy trust

Since your reputation is largely based on your ability to meet your commitments to others, especially early in your career, it's important that you meet your commitments 100% of the time. It only takes one missed commitment to damage your reputation.

In the event that extenuating circumstances will prevent you from meeting a commitment, it's important that you let your stakeholders know as soon as possible and always <u>before the due date</u>. This allows you to make a new commitment, and gives your stakeholders time to react to the missed commitment; including resetting whatever commitments they may have made based on your commitment.

68

Owners beg for forgiveness, not ask for permission

"Owners" take accountability for outcomes. "Workers" on the other hand, may put in the time but have no sense of responsibility for their work, the work of the team, or the business. You want to behave like an owner.

One attribute of owners is that when they see a problem or an opportunity they dive in to address it. They don't run to their boss to ask for permission to solve the issue. Instead, they'll do what they believe needs to be done in the best interest of the business, and if they're wrong, they "beg for forgiveness" after the fact.

Of course, this strategy requires that as an owner, you have good judgement, especially in terms of determining what is important and right to you, your boss, and your company.

69

You have to enjoy the ride

There are no happy endings.
Endings are the saddest part,
So just give me a happy middle
And a very happy start.

-   Shel Silverstein

It's really easy to spend your working days waiting to retire. Imagine how great it will be when you no longer have to work!

The average career is much, much too long to think like that. Of course, there will be good days and bad days, but on average you need to find enjoyment in your work. If you don't enjoy it on the whole, perhaps you are in the wrong job.

It's not about the destination of retirement. It's about the journey of your career. Enjoy the journey.

70

Vacations are required

One piece of advice that I received early in my career is that you should always either be on vacation, or planning one. It's good advice.

Vacations:

- allow you to recharge and reenergize
- break up the monotony
- help you keep perspective
- force you to be a team player (if you are a one-person show, you will never be able to get away)
- make you more productive
- make you more innovative
- make you a more interesting person

Consider vacations required.

71

You should embrace change

"The secret of change is to focus all of your energy, not on fighting the old, but on building the new."

- Excerpt from *Way of the Peaceful Warrior: A Book that Changes Lives* by Dan Millman

In the workplace, change happens all the time. Companies are bought, sold, merged, and divested. Organizations are augmented, restructured, and right-sized. Strategies are reimagined and processes are re-engineered. People are promoted, transitioned, and replaced. Truly, the only constant in business is change.

People largely react to change in one of two ways:

- They will <u>resist</u> change because change is hard, disruptive, and creates uncertainty.
- They will <u>embrace</u> change because change is evolutionary and opens up new opportunities.

It's important that you be one of those people who embraces change. There are three main reasons why:

- Resisting change makes the change even more painful. You spend your time focused on the negative, wallowing in what could have been.
- Resisting change is a waste of time. Change is the natural order of our universe. You aren't going to stop or reverse the change.
- The people that embrace the change the soonest are the people that are most likely to benefit from the opportunities that the change presents. For example, if new positions or promotions open up in support of the changed organization, who is going to move into those roles? Will it be the resister or the embracer?

In summary, embrace change. Don't resist it.

72

You should always be relevant

It's easy to fall into the trap of "dumb, fat, and happy." Don't. The workplace is constantly changing, and if you aren't paying attention to it, it's easy to get caught on the wrong side of the skills curve. Imagine:

- being a telephone operator with the invention of automated switches
- working at Blockbuster when video-on-demand was invented
- being a travel agent when the Internet made travel self-service
- being a taxi driver when Uber was created
- being a software developer proficient in an ancient language like COBOL
- being a truck driver in the upcoming world of driverless cars

I would argue that these folks had plenty of time to see the changes coming. The problem is that many people didn't do anything about it.

Usually the issue of becoming irrelevant is not quite so obvious. The hard skills you use on your job today are almost certainly not going to be the same skills you need throughout your career (soft interpersonal skills, on the other hand, should be useful throughout your working life).

On top of that, relevancy is really on a spectrum; it's not like you are either relevant or not. The question is <u>how</u> relevant are your knowledge, experiences, and skills to your customers, your bosses, and your colleagues.

The more relevant you are, the more opportunities for success that will be available to you.

73

You should never stop learning

School is over but learning never stops. In order to stay relevant, you need to constantly be learning new things. Some of those learnings will be new hard skills, some will be new soft (interpersonal) skills, and some of those learnings may be on seemingly unrelated topics to your work life. Even those unrelated topics will help you at work, in terms of being innovative. Innovation is often the connection of unrelated ideas in new ways.

Take advantage of training that is offered by your employer, but don't stop there. Research training and certifications that are either interesting or relevant to your career, and pursue them.

74

It's important to know how to handle a bad role

On occasion you will find yourself in a "bad" role (position) at work. The role may be bad because it is boring or unsatisfying. It may be bad because you have a bad boss, or a lack of coaching, direction, and oversight. Sometimes even a good role can become a bad role if things change or if you have been in the role too long.

Here are some tips for dealing with a "bad" role:

- Figure out what you can learn from the role. Often what makes a role bad is a lack of opportunities to learn and grow. There is nearly always something that you can learn from a role, even if it's what not to do.
- Fix the role. Don't assume the role is the role, and there's nothing you can do about it. Sometimes, if you can figure out what is making you unhappy, you can reshape the role to address the issue.
- Time-box the role. Usually you can't get out of a bad role right away, but almost always you can put time constraints around it. Have a candid discussion with your boss or others in the organization around setting a

timeframe when you'll be able to move to something else.

- Find your next role. You don't want to be perceived as "running away" from a role. Instead, identify the next great opportunity and use that as the reason to have a conversation with your boss about time-boxing your current role so that you can take advantage of your next potential role.

Occasionally finding yourself in a bad role is unavoidable. But it's important that you know how to handle it.

YOUR BOSS: BECOMING SUCCESSFUL TOGETHER

75

Bosses and peers need to be managed

Your bosses and peers have a lot of influence on your work. They also may or may not share your perspective on what is important. It would be disastrous to ignore work that your boss thinks is important or to spend your time on that which he thinks is unimportant. It can also be disastrous to ignore activities that are not important to you, but that support critical activities for your coworkers.

Therefore you need to be able to:

- Articulate what's important and why
- Articulate what's not important and why
- Understand what's important to your boss and why
- Understand what's important to your coworkers and why
- Balance your agenda with the agenda of your boss and coworkers
- Wherever possible, align your agenda with that of your boss and/or coworkers (which makes sense, since you are all on the same team in pursuit of presumably the same overall goal)

It's important to learn how to manage upwards and sideways.

76

Your success is tied to your boss' success

Just like making your customer successful will make you successful; so it is with your boss. If you can understand what success looks like for your boss, and align your measures of success to your boss' measures, you will be well positioned to be successful in the organization.

It sounds simple, but there are a few things that can be challenging:

- You need to understand what success looks like for your boss. Sometimes you can figure it out by their role; otherwise, you should ask her.
- Often, you have more than one "boss." In these cases, you need to figure out how to make all of them successful.
- You need to figure out how what you do in your role can best contribute to your boss' success.

77

Surprises suck

Adopt a "no surprises" philosophy with your boss and colleagues. "No Surprises" means that you notify your stakeholders at the first sign of a potential issue. The last thing you want to do is have your boss, customer, or colleague surprised by an issue that they didn't know was coming. If you don't see an issue coming until it's too late, at least ensure that your boss hears about the issue from you, as opposed to a customer or one of his peers in the organization.

No surprises!

78

You should bring solutions, not problems

"Remember that complaining about a problem without proposing a solution is called 'whining'"

- Teddy Roosevelt

Throughout your career, you will need to report status and escalate issues to your bosses. Keep in mind that your boss is not there to solve your problems. Your boss is there to help you think through and decide on options, to knock down obstacles that are outside of your control, to obtain resources that you need to be successful, and to advocate on your behalf to others.

When you experience a problem, you don't necessarily need to have the exact solution, but you should always bring well thought out options to your boss, along with your specific asks of them.

79

Leaders have different styles

There are an infinite number of different leadership styles, and over the course of your career, you'll be exposed to a myriad of different styles. Some styles you will connect with instantly because it matches how you like to work and other styles will be more difficult.

Some leaders will micro-manage while other leaders will give you a lot of autonomy. Some leaders like to touch base informally multiple times a day and some leaders like to communicate more formally on a less frequent basis, perhaps through a written status report. Some leaders speak candidly, some sugarcoat everything. Some leaders are very egalitarian, some are very hierarchical.

Whenever you get a new boss, it's important that you understand their style and preferences as quickly as possible. The sooner you can understand how they like to work, the better you will work together. In my experience, the easiest approach is to directly talk with your new boss at the first meeting about how he likes to work, and how he would like you to interact with him.

80

Employees must adapt upward

Regardless of your manager's style or your own style, it is incumbent on you to adapt to working with your boss. Employees adapt to their managers; not the other way around.

If you try and stick to how you like to work when your boss doesn't like to work that way, it is almost certainly going to lead to friction in the relationship, and potentially bad performance reviews when your boss feels like you are difficult to work with.

Adapt your style to match your manager's.

81

Outworking your boss sends a good message

Ideally, you get to work before your manager and you leave after her. This sends the message that you are not afraid of hard work and that you are fully committed to the job and your career.

Likewise, responding to e-mails or phone calls after hours and on weekends reinforces your commitment and your work ethic. Being a dedicated, hard-working employee is an oft cited piece of positive feedback, and completely within your control.

82

Bosses love initiative

If you have some extra time on your hands, seek out your manager and ask him if there is anything you can help him with. This shows initiative, commitment, and dedication; and often will differentiate you from your peers. Even if he doesn't have anything for you to do, he now knows that you are willing to take on additional responsibilities if something should come along.

83

Receiving feedback is an important skill

Self-improvement is a lifetime pursuit. Even the best in their field at the peak of their success; Tiger Woods in golf and Michael Jordan in basketball; worked diligently and tirelessly with their coaches to continually improve.

A very important tool in your professional development is performance feedback. Feedback will come from a variety of sources: your boss, your colleagues, and even the people who work for you. Every piece of feedback is a gift.

Receiving feedback can be difficult. If it's positive feedback, you may feel embarrassed by the perceived flattery. If it's negative feedback, you will likely feel hurt and defensive. It's important to know how to graciously accept and apply performance feedback. Here are some tips:

- Picture yourself outside of the situation. The overall goal is to <u>objectively</u> understand, assess, and apply the feedback. It's difficult to be objective when the feedback is about you; being "outside of yourself" can help.
- Remember that negative feedback is often more useful to your professional development than positive feedback.

- Use active listening techniques. This will ensure you collect all of the data you need to understand and assess the feedback, and it will demonstrate to the person providing the feedback that you are genuinely interested in hearing it.

- Don't argue the feedback. Fight your natural tendency to defend yourself or provide explanation, unless it will help you better your understanding of the feedback. The problem is that even if you are right and the feedback is off-base, defending yourself can be interpreted as you being unreceptive or not coachable. Also keep in mind that sometimes perception is reality.

- Thank the person providing the feedback. Remember that feedback is a gift.

- Spend a day or more afterwards thinking objectively about the feedback you received. Why did the person giving the feedback think like they did? Was the feedback valid? Have you heard it before, maybe in a different way? What could or should you have done differently?

- Apply the feedback. The feedback only really has value if it helps your professional or personal development. A valuable tool for this purpose is "Start, Stop, Continue." Based on the feedback, what should you start doing; what should you stop doing; and what should you continue doing?

Learn to receive feedback and it will benefit you throughout your career.

MANAGING EXPECTATIONS: BASELINES MATTER

84

Success is always measured as results against expectations

Scenarios like this happen all the time... You're proud and excited about the deliverable that you've created; it's even on-time and on-budget! You show it to the client... and they hate it. What?!

Success isn't about results. It's about results <u>as measured against expectations</u>. It doesn't matter how great your work is, if your boss or client was expecting better, they will be underwhelmed. On the flip side, your work could be mediocre, but if your stakeholders were expecting less, they will be impressed.

Very, very often in the work setting, failures are a function of expectations; not a function of results. You have to be good at managing both.

85

All business is show business

Businesses are run by people and people like a good show. Often, producing good business impact isn't enough – the presentation also needs to impress.

Your customer's experience with you and your company is a part of what they are purchasing from your company. So not just the product you are producing needs to exceed their expectations; their view of the whole experience needs to exceed their expectations.

The customer experience includes:

- Meetings
- Phone calls
- After-hours events
- E-mails
- Branding
- Office space
- Interaction with customer service
- Etc.

The key is to remember that you need to put your company's best foot forward at every interaction, not just in the final product.

86

Perception often is reality

Sometimes, clients and colleagues will have a perception that isn't based on reality. For example, perhaps a customer believes you are unresponsive because she tried to contact you, but your e-mail server was down and she dialed the wrong phone number. She may believe that you don't care about her business and that you have more important customers that you care more about.

The fact that her belief is incorrect doesn't matter. What matters is that she now believes you aren't responsive and you don't care about her business. The issues that the e-mail server was down and that she has a wrong phone number for you are superfluous. The real issue is now her perception. Her perception is the reality that matters.

This actually happens a lot. Your natural instinct will be to debunk the perception, and it is important to set the record straight; but the more important thing is to acknowledge that perception is reality, and that you have a perception issue to address.

Here is how you address it:

- Where possible without flaming the fire, make sure the perceiver understands what really happened. Don't be defensive, just get the facts out on the table.
- Acknowledge that you understand how she could have had that perception.
- Fix the perception issue (separate from the real issue). For example, if the perception is that you don't care about the customer, get on a plane, go take her to dinner, and renew your commitment.

87

Expectations need to be managed early and often

You shouldn't let expectations just happen. You need to proactively manage them. That is how you can ensure that you don't end up surprised when you deliver your final results to a disappointed stakeholder. The key is to manage expectations as early on as possible, and constantly revisit expectations throughout.

It's not as hard as it sounds. There are some simple things you can do to help manage expectations:

- Don't over-promise.
- Ask your stakeholders what they are expecting. One common way to ask this question is in the form of "what do you think success looks like?"
- Share intermediate deliverables or samples as early as possible and as often as possible.
- Remind your stakeholders what to expect; even in terms of the bad stuff that might accompany the good.

Manage expectations early. Manage expectations often.

THE WORKPLACE: KEEPING IT PROFESSIONAL

88

Companies have personalities

Each company has its own distinct "personality", commonly referred to as "culture." Culture cannot be quantified and often it's even difficult to describe. But it differs wildly between companies. Cultures can feel entrepreneurial, stiff, relaxed, competitive, inclusive, cliquey, unprofessional, arrogant, old, young, loud, quiet, results-oriented, time-oriented, etc., etc., etc. Thinking of culture as a company's personality is appropriate, because they can be just as varied as the personalities of people.

Interestingly, it's nearly impossible to implement a specific culture. Just like an individual personality, it forms on its own as a function of a nearly infinite number of inputs. Corporate culture is defined by the type of people that work there, the leaders throughout the organization, the policies and practices of the company, corporate strategies and goals, the physical work environment, and a myriad of other things.

Obviously you both influence and are influenced by the company culture, but the important thing is that you need to feel like you "fit" within the culture. If you find that you aren't a good fit within your company's culture, you may want to look for another job. It's just too difficult to be happy and successful in a company culture that you don't fit with.

89

You should dress for the job you want

One part of culture is attire. You should dress consistently with the culture of your workplace. If your workplace is dressy business attire, dress up. If it's business casual, wear business casual.

That said, there will likely be some variability in how people dress in the workplace. Some people may dress more casually while others dress more professionally. A good guideline is to dress for the job you want, not the job you have.

If your colleagues are all wearing jeans to work, but your boss wears dress slacks, consider wearing slacks. Here's why: people at work will draw conclusions about your competence, potential, and professional status based in part on what you wear.

90

When in doubt, you should over-dress

If you don't know what to wear, always opt to over-dress. If you are wearing a suit while everyone else is in jeans, it's fine. It just comes across as either you felt like dressing up, or that you are trying to look more professional. However, if you wear jeans when everyone else is wearing suits, it comes across as if you don't care or don't get it.

91

After-hours work events are still work events

In the course of your career, you may have hundreds, if not thousands, of after-hours work events. These could range from informal drinks with coworkers after work to formal dinners with customers. Regardless of the formality or the setting, never forget that <u>interactions with coworkers and customers, even outside of work, are work events</u>.

That doesn't mean you can't be friends with your coworkers. You can and should be friends with the people you work with; you spend at least half of your waking hours in their company. But friends or not, you have to be able to work with these folks. And whether or not you or they deliberately make judgements surrounding people's behavior outside of work, it does infiltrate your reputation in the work place.

If you have too much to drink, or if you hit on one of your colleagues, the timing or setting doesn't matter. It will impact how your coworkers view you once you return to your desk.

PROFESSIONAL RELATIONSHIPS: REQUIRED FOR SUCCESS

92

Networking is a part of the job

Work is a team sport. You can't be successful by yourself; you need to have strong professional relationships to help you along the way. In addition, building relationships doesn't happen automatically. It's something you have to work at.

Here are some tips for successful networking:

- Make it a habit to walk around and talk to people at work.
- Go to lunch with someone every chance you get.
- Go out after work.
- Leverage LinkedIn.
- Never turn down an opportunity to meet someone you don't know. You never know where that connection might lead.
- Keep your connections warm. If you haven't talked to someone in a long time, go grab coffee or at least drop them an e-mail to catch up. If they live out-of-town, and you happen to be traveling to their city, look them up and grab coffee or a drink after work.

In summary, remember that networking is a part of the job.

93

Remembering names matters

Using someone's name is a sign of intimacy. When you use someone's name, it shows that you care about them as a person. But unless you are one of those people who has a natural knack for remembering faces and names, you will have to work at this.

Here are some tips for remembering names:

- When someone introduces themselves, repeat their name back to them; which will help you remember.
- After you meet someone and they walk away, spend a minute by yourself to memorize their name. An even more effective memorization technique is to write down their name, perhaps even with a note or description that will help you remember them.
- Use names as much as possible when you talk to folks around the office. It promotes professional intimacy and will further reinforce names in your memory.

Remembering names is important.

94

You should always be genuine

People are exceptionally good at recognizing when someone is being disingenuous. Folks that aren't genuine in the workplace come across as duplicitous, slimy, or as "brown-nosers." People don't want to work with or for people like this.

Be the best you at work, but always be you.

95

Diversity has a population of one

At work, the term 'diversity' will often be used in terms of ethnicity, gender, age, sexual orientation, etc. As it relates to corporate responsibility and macro-level issues of diversity, this definition makes sense.

However, this is a very narrow view of diversity as it relates to professional relationships. For example, it would be incorrect and short-sighted to think that all African-American women have the same needs, wants, behaviors, and beliefs at work; and to interact with them all in an identical way.

In reality, every individual in the workplace represents a diversity of one. Each person is their own individual, unlike any other individual, and more diverse than any diversity grouping that can be defined. Understand each person as an individual, and it will go a very long way in terms of developing meaningful, long-lasting relationships.

96

The Golden Rule
is wrong

The Golden Rule states that you should do unto others as you would have them do unto you. The Golden Rule is wrong!

You shouldn't treat others as <u>you</u> want to be treated. You should treat others as <u>they</u> want to be treated.

Every person is a diversity of one. Everyone you work with will have their own individual way of working and unique style of communicating. It's important that you be able to adapt how you interact with others to match how each individual best responds. For example, if one of your colleagues' communication style is short and direct; a long and verbose explanation of an issue is probably not the most effective way to connect with him; even if that's how you prefer to communicate.

Treat each individual according to how they want to be treated.

97

Roles change suddenly

Imagine this scenario. Work is going great. You're working on a fantastic project, sponsored by the company's Chief Financial Officer (CFO). You've been working on the project for almost 18 months, the CFO loves your work, and you're virtually assured a promotion when the project ends. Then, a few weeks before the end of the project, the Chief Executive Officer (CEO) gets replaced by the Board of Directors. The new CEO brings in his own executive team, including a new CFO, who doesn't value the project and decides to shut it down. All of a sudden, your biggest fan is no longer with the company, your project has ended, and you don't know where (or to whom) to go next.

Implausible? It actually happens all the time. People, including you, will have their roles change suddenly. In addition, when new people come into a new role, they will generally bring in other new individuals that they already know and trust from their old role. This creates a "domino effect" that can impact a lot of people in the organization.

There are two specific things you can do to protect yourself from these kinds of sudden role changes:

- Pay attention! Don't become "dumb, fat, and happy" in your current role. Keep an eye on the dynamics in the broader organization and with your boss' relationships with his boss and his peers. More often than not, you can see the change coming if you are paying attention.

- Make sure you have a broad network. If you have all of your eggs in one basket, what do you do if that "basket" leaves the company? Having strong relationships with people at different levels in different parts of the organization, can be very useful in times of change.

Roles change suddenly. You need to be prepared.

COMMUNICATION: THE LIFE-BLOOD OF BUSINESS

98

Work is a team sport

Imagine the running back on a football team trying to get anywhere without his teammates all doing their jobs in a coordinated way. Now try and imagine those 11 players trying to coordinate movements without being able to communicate amongst themselves via verbal instructions or play calling. It would be unproductive chaos. As it is with work. Your team can't be successful without effective communication.

Since team communication boils down to individual communication, it's imperative that you are an effective communicator. While it may seem that communication is an inherent skill that you're born with, it's actually not. It's a skill that requires deliberate practice.

Work is a team sport, and everyone needs to communicate effectively for the company to be effective. When in doubt, it's better to over communicate than under communicate.

99

In terms of collaboration, one plus one equals three

An extension of communication is collaboration, the action of working together with someone to co-create or co-decide on something.

An interesting phenomenon regarding collaboration is that often the pair (or group) of people that are collaborating will leave the discussion with an idea or decision that is completely different from the ideas or decisions that either person brought into the discussion.

This concept is extremely powerful, because it means the output of a collaboration is greater than the sum of the individual contributors. As each contributor presents their ideas or points-of-view, other contributors are able to build and tweak upon them, ultimately leading to a better place than any contributor would have come to on their own.

Collaboration will nearly always yield a better solution than not collaborating. Collaborate early and often.

100

Collaboration can save your job

Collaboration can literally save your job.

In the course of your career, you are occasionally going to make mistakes. Your business judgment will not be flawless, and you are sometimes going to make the wrong decision. In the instance where you make a decision by yourself, without collaboration, you can't hide from the consequences of your poor judgement. By contrast, if you collaborated with others on the decision, even if it is the wrong decision, following the right process and testing your thinking with others is usually enough to chalk it up to a simple mistake.

Said another way, try and avoid being out on a limb by yourself. Collaboration with others protects everyone.

101

You need to learn to read people

Communication is much more than what people say. Body language and tone-of-voice are critically important indicators of what people think and how they feel. A huge part of working effectively with others is being able to read these non-verbal cues.

Reading people is important because it gives you an opportunity to change your message or your delivery to be more effective. It also can provide important clues about what the other person is thinking, or if there are hidden agendas and motives in play. For example, if you are sitting in a meeting and you notice that one client subtly bristles at the comment from one of her colleagues, that could indicate an organizational dynamic that you need to be aware of in working with the client.

Reading people is an important skill that improves with practice.

102

How you communicate matters

I had a manager early in my career tell me that, "regardless of the message, you can make someone feel any way you want them to feel." While the phrasing can certainly make it sound manipulative, the advice is very insightful. Effectively, it says that you can and should separate the message from the delivery.

Consider these two potential approaches to delivering the same message:

- "John, that presentation that was due next week now needs to be in the customer's hands tomorrow."
- "John, I know you've been killing it lately, but Mary is in a bind and needs that presentation in her hands tomorrow instead of next week. What can we do to help her out?"

Both examples deliver the same message: "the deadline got moved up." However, how the message will be received is likely to be very different.

Remember that how you communicate is often more important than what you communicate.

103

It's usually best to listen first and speak second

As human beings, our natural tendency is to speak. There are some very significant advantages to suppressing this natural tendency, and ensuring we listen and understand, before we speak.

These advantages include:

- avoiding jumping to a premature conclusion because you don't have all of the facts
- providing the ability to tailor your message or your delivery to your audience, since you'll better understand their current point-of-view
- making the other person more receptive to listening to you, since you listened to them
- allowing you to make the concluding statement in the conversation, if appropriate

Listen first. Speak second.

104

Active listening is a skill

We've been listening to other people talk since birth, so we must really be good at listening at this point, right?

Actually, human beings are generally terrible at listening. Often when people talk to each other, they are distracted, half-listening, or thinking about what they are going to say next.

Active listening refers to a specific technique that can be taught and is incredibly useful in the workplace in terms of improving communication and collaboration.

At a very high-level, active listening consists of:

- paying very close attention to what a person is saying and how they are saying it
- demonstrating that you are listening through body language (nodding) or verbal acknowledgements
- playing back what they are saying to ensure that you have a common understanding of what they are trying to say

It's worthwhile to practice active listening at work.

105

Crisp is clear

In general, the business world likes crisp, clear communication.

Being verbose in the workplace can lead to ambiguity, tries people's patience, and washes out the key message(s).

In addition, people who have a history of being verbose are often not taken as seriously as someone who uses crisp, direct language. Think about it, if someone doesn't speak that often, people have a tendency to listen more when they speak. Also, people that speak crisply appear more confident.

If you do have a tendency to be verbose, there are some things you can do to work on it:

- Try and speak up every other time that you feel the need to speak.
- When someone asks you a question, answer the question directly first, then elaborate. For example, "Yes. But the status is complicated because..."
- Avoid redundancy. If you've already said it, there is no need to say it again with different words unless you get the indication that people didn't understand you the first time.

In summary, the power of your words is inversely proportional to the number of words you use.

NEGOTIATION: SCIENCE, NOT ART

106

Negotiation is a skill

Negotiation, in its broadest sense, refers to your ability to persuade, convince, and drive agreement with colleagues, supervisors, clients, and vendors. In this broad definition, negotiation isn't something isolated to leaders in your organization. It's applicable to all employees from the day they begin working.

Despite the connotation that the word has to many people, negotiation is also not a dark art practiced exclusively by slimy used car salesmen in plaid sports coats. Negotiation is a valuable business skill, with tried-and-true techniques, that can be improved with practice.

107

You should always seek to understand "why"

There is a common anecdote of two sisters who see one orange on the kitchen table, and argue about who gets it. In the course of their negotiation, they decide to just cut the orange in half. At that point, the first sister eats her half of the orange, throws the peel away, and is still hungry. Meanwhile, the other sister throws her half of the orange away and grates the peel into orange zest for half of her muffin recipe. While it would seem like splitting the orange in half is a fair resolution to the negotiation, it's actually a huge negotiation fail. Both sisters could have gotten exactly what they wanted, but instead neither got what they wanted.[4]

What was the failure in this negotiation? Neither sister tried to understand why the other sister wanted the orange.

Step one in any negotiation or attempt to persuade is to understand the other person's underlying motive. Why do they want what they want or believe what they believe? If you understand this, it becomes much easier to negotiate to a resolution that both parties can live with.

---

[4] The story of the two sisters and the orange is attributed to Mary Parker Follett, one of the pioneers of management theory.

108

It's important to find common ground

Almost always, there is common ground. The trick in any negotiation is to figure out what it is, so that you can anchor back to what both parties want, before you worry about what each individual wants.

Here are some examples of finding common ground:

- "Mr. Client, we're both interested in the same thing; we want the project to be on-time and on-budget."
- "Fellow Team Lead, we both want the same thing; we want to make sure that neither one of our teams gets burned out by working a lot of weekends."
- "Miss Coworker, I think we both are looking for the same thing; we would like to work in a less stressful environment so we can enjoy work more."
- "Mr. Vendor, we both want the same outcome; you want to sell me your software, and I want to buy your software."

Statements like these can diffuse difficult negotiations and help make the negotiation productive by anchoring it to a common goal.

109

Balance of power matters

Negotiations are only balanced when the relative power of the parties negotiating is balanced. That doesn't mean that you only negotiate when on level ground with the other party. It does however, mean that you need to understand the balance of power to be effective in the negotiation. If you have less power in the negotiation, you may need to compromise more than the other party.

Consider these examples of imbalanced negotiations:

- an athlete negotiating a call with a referee
- a student negotiating a grade with a teacher
- a poorly performing employee negotiating a raise with his manager
- a high performing employee with critical skills negotiating a raise with his manager
- a large, successful consulting firm with lots of clients negotiating price with a small client
- a large customer representing a large portion of a vendor's business negotiating price with the vendor

Balance of power matters.

110

You need to understand your BATNA

BATNA stands for Best Alternative to a Negotiated Agreement. The acronym was developed by Roger Fisher and William Ury in their 1981 book, *Getting to Yes: Negotiating Without Giving In.* In essence, understanding your BATNA means understanding your best option if can't get to an agreement with the other party.

It's important to understand your BATNA prior to entering any negotiation because it defines your backup plan, or your worst case scenario if negotiations fail. This knowledge helps you ensure that you always negotiate better than worst case, and it also may give you more leverage, or power in the negotiation. For example, if you know you can go buy a new mobile phone on-line for $200, you wouldn't settle for any price higher than that when negotiating with the sales person at the store.

MANAGEMENT AND LEADERSHIP: IT'S ABOUT PEOPLE

111

Leaders have followers

Thousands of books have been written on the topic of leadership, each with its own definition of leadership and point-of-view on what makes effective leaders. Many of these are great books, worthy of reading. The challenge is that there is no single recipe for leadership; leaders come in all shapes, sizes, and styles.

One common denominator of all leaders is that leaders have followers. Followers are not the same as direct reports, nor are they the same as people who follow a leader out of fear or intimidation. Followers refer to a group of people that choose of their own free-will to be led by an individual.

The ultimate litmus test for leadership is to understand if there are people that are willing to follow that person. This has little to do with organizational structure. There are plenty of managers who are not leaders, and plenty of individual contributors without direct reports, who are great leaders.

112

All people are intrinsically motivated by the same things

Daniel Pink deciphers human motivation in his 2009 book, *Drive: The Surprising Truth About What Motivates Us*. What he concludes is that human beings are all, by nature, intrinsically motivated by three things: autonomy, mastery, and purpose. Autonomy refers to our desire to be self-directed; mastery refers to our desire to learn and improve our skills; and purpose refers to our desire to do something meaningful.

Without summarizing the whole book (it's a fantastic book), the important thing to remember is that people are intrinsically motivated by autonomy, mastery, and purpose; and if you are able to provide this for the folks that you lead, they will go further than if you rely upon extrinsic motivations like money.

113

Responsibilities should be delegated; not tasks

"If you want to build a ship, don't drum up people to collect wood and don't assign them tasks and work, but rather teach them to long for the endless immensity of the sea."

- Antoine de Saint-Exupery

Many managers tell their subordinates what to do. This is usually referred to as micro-management. However, great managers don't micro-manage, they delegate scopes of responsibilities as opposed to individual tasks.

Since we know that people are intrinsically motivated by autonomy, it makes sense that folks are both happier and more productive when they have ownership over the creative process as opposed to having every task and activity dictated to them.

114

Only the committed can commit

A commitment is a promise to do or give something. It isn't possible to commit (i.e. make a promise) on the behalf of someone else. Certainly managers can and often do commit other people to work and timelines all the time. But that's a different level of commitment. Really it's a false commitment. Consider these two scenarios:

- A manager tells the customer that a programmer on his team will have his work done by Monday.
- The programmer tells his manager that he will have his work done by Monday.

When the programmer runs into difficulty and has to work the weekend to get it all done, in which scenario is he more likely to deliver? Is he more likely to deliver against his manager's commitment or his own?

As a leader, if you want your people to deliver on their promises, you need to allow them to control the promises.

115

Great leaders are like umbrellas

In the same theme as doing what's best for your customers and what's best for your boss; great leaders tend to put their followers first.

Great leaders are like umbrellas.

In stormy times, when clients are angry or times are uncertain, great leaders open up like an umbrella to protect their teams. They take full accountability for issues, they encapsulate their teams from the noise and uncertainty, and they allow their teams to focus on getting their work done.

In sunny times, when praise is flowing from clients or company leadership, great leaders close like an umbrella and get out of the way so that the team can bask in the sun and celebrate their success. Great leaders know that they don't need to bask in success. Success of the leader is measured on the success of their teams.

116

All volunteers are good volunteers

You should never say no to a volunteer (although you may need to redirect them). As a leader in an organization, people will come to you with ideas that they'd like the organization to implement. Passion is very powerful; if someone has enough passion around an issue or opportunity to bring it to you, it's likely that they will have the passion to do a good job implementing the solution.

Here are some tips regarding volunteers:

- If someone brings an issue to you, ask them to take ownership of solving it. More often than not, they will agree to solve it because it's something they obviously care about. Worst case scenario, they will learn to not bring problems without solutions.
- If someone volunteers to help with something, always take them up on it.
- If you don't agree with the idea, feel free to tweak it, but don't kill it altogether. The trick is to harness the passion, not squelch it.

117

Giving feedback is an important skill

As a leader, giving meaningful, constructive, and timely feedback is an important part of your job. Amongst other things, you are responsible for the professional development of the people on your teams. Here are some tips for giving effective feedback:

- Give feedback often. The more often you provide feedback (positive and negative), the more comfortable your team members will be receiving the feedback.

- Give feedback as close to the event that initiated the feedback as possible. For example, after an important client meeting, I usually provide feedback (positive and negative) to members of my team immediately afterwards.

- Always provide individual feedback in private. Remember that receiving feedback is difficult; don't make it more difficult by making it a public event. Positive feedback that applies to the whole group (not individual feedback) can and should be shared publically with the group.

- Ensure that the feedback is specific and based on an observable event, not on your judgment of the event. For example, the feedback would be, "you spent 15 minutes getting the presentation ready at the beginning of the meeting"; not "you came into the meeting unprepared" (that would be a judgment that may or may not be the underlying cause of the presentation not being ready when the meeting started).

- Balance positive and negative feedback. If you are constantly telling people how great they are and never what they have to work on, your feedback will be dismissed as superficial. At the other extreme, if you are constantly giving negative feedback without any positive feedback, your team will perceive you as "impossible to please" and your negative feedback will be dismissed as noise.

- Be candid. Don't sugarcoat feedback. Be clear and concise, and avoid using superfluous language. People have a tendency to hear what they want to hear, so if you put flowery language around negative feedback, they will miss the point.

- Don't be mean. You can be candid and direct without being mean. Be compassionate when giving feedback. Remember that receiving feedback is difficult, and that both you and your team member are focused on the same objective – you want him to develop professionally.

- If you receive feedback about one of your team members from another person, be sure to share it with the team member. If you have feedback for a member of another team, deliver it directly to that team member. If the feedback is positive, deliver it to the team member and make sure their supervisor hears it as well.

Giving feedback is an important skill you will need throughout your career.

JOB SECURITY: YOUR JOB, YOUR PROBLEM

118

Job security is not the responsibility of your employer

Perhaps fifty years ago, companies felt a loyalty to their employees (and vice versa) culminating in an employee spending 40 years with the same company, retiring, and getting a watch. Or perhaps even that is just a figment of nostalgia. Either way, in today's world, you can't rely on company loyalty for your job security.

Your employer is responsible for providing you a safe working environment and generating profits for their stakeholders. That is where their obligations end.

It's not your employer's responsibility to provide you job security.

119

Job security is a function of your value to the company

The best way to obtain job security at your company is to be as valuable as possible to your company. You can think of your value to the company in terms of relevance and impact.

In terms of relevance, are you working within a critical department with meaningful impact to the profitability of the company? Do you have skills that are relevant to the profitability and/or strategy of the company?

In terms of impact, are you a high-performing employee? Do the company leaders, your manager, and your coworkers think that you are a high-performing employee? Do you have measurable, quantifiable impact on the profits of the company?

When it comes to job security, it doesn't benefit you to lie to yourself with these questions. Be intellectually honest with yourself, and if the answer to any of these questions is "no" then you have some work to do to increase your relevance and impact.

120

Job security is a function of your value to the market

While we often think about job security in terms of the security of your current job, a broader definition would also include your ability to get a new job in the open market.

Just like your value within your current company, your value in the open market is largely a function of your relevance within your industry. It is also a function of your potential impact as determined by the network of people that know your work and are now working at other companies.

You have control over your relevance and perceived potential impact in the market. Here are some ideas:

- Keep up your market relevance by staying on top of industry trends and participating in training.
- Publish market-facing whitepapers and/or points-of-view in industry publications, or in conjunction with your company's website or personal blog.
- Maintain a strong network.

121

Job security is a function of your network

The majority of jobs today are filled by referral.

Certainly it's possible to find a job by blindly applying and competing with hundreds of other applicants, but it's much, much, much easier to find jobs through your professional network.

As your career progresses, your network will become larger, and people in your network will move around from company to company. If you do your job maintaining your network, this can become a very powerful security blanket if and when you are looking for a new job.

In short, the more people in the market that know you and trust you, the more people that are willing to refer you or hire you.

122

Your résumé should always be up to date

Some people put their résumé on ice as soon as they get a job, and they don't worry about it again until they need or want a new job. I don't recommend that approach. You are better off keeping your résumé up-to-date.

First of all, it's easier to keep your résumé up-to-date as you go because it's harder to go back and remember all of your roles and accomplishments after a lot of time passes.

Second, if you suddenly find yourself wanting a new job because you are unhappy in your current job, because a great opportunity comes up, or because you lose your job; time matters. You want to have that résumé ready so that you can react quickly.

Lastly, having an updated résumé always available to the market (for example, via LinkedIn), can lead to opportunities that you wouldn't otherwise be made aware of, since recruiters use résumés as the primary method for identifying candidates.

123

There is a right way to quit

There is a right way and a wrong way to quit. The market within your industry in your area can be surprisingly small. As such it can be very likely that you will cross paths with people you worked with at one job in another job. Or you may cross paths when someone you used to work with becomes a customer. Therefore, the last thing you want to do is unnecessarily burn bridges when you quit.

This is the right way to quit:

- Once you have the other offer in hand (but not before), and before you accept the new offer, give your boss the professional courtesy of letting them know that you are looking to leave. This can be controversial, but I believe you should give your boss the opportunity to fix what might be driving you to leave and/or make a counter-offer.
- As soon as you accept the new offer, provide notice of your resignation in writing (email is fine) to your boss and to your Human Resources representative.
- Include in your resignation letter your preferred last day with the company. Provide at least two weeks' notice, and preferably more; your company will appreciate any

flexibility you can give them, and again, the idea is to leave on the best possible terms.

- Reach out personally to people that you have a personal relationship with, as many as you can, to let them know that you resigned. It's best for them to hear it from you.
- On your last day, send a well written, kind, and professional e-mail to your network of coworkers, thanking them for the privilege of working with them.

In summary, always quit with professionalism and dignity. You will most likely work with some of these people again.

124

There is a right time to quit

Changing jobs is a big decision. Don't make it on a whim. I received a good piece of advice early in my career: "Only quit on a good day."

In your work life, you will have plenty of good days and plenty of bad days. It would be a mistake to boil down your job to how you feel on any particular day. By making sure you only quit on a good day, you ensure that you aren't making a rash decision based on a transient feeling.

TRAVEL

Whether you are traveling for work or for pleasure, travel can be an excruciating process or a pleasant escape. Here are some things to know that will hopefully give you less of the former and more of the latter.

TRAVEL REWARDS: MEMBERSHIP HAS ITS PRIVILEGES

125

It's worthwhile to register for loyalty programs

Frequent traveler programs (airline, hotel, car, and train) are easy to sign up for, valuable, and can actually be fun. Whenever you are traveling with a new airline, staying at a new hotel, or renting a car from a new car rental company, spend five minutes to register for their loyalty program so that you can maximize the benefits of the trip.

The benefits of frequent traveler programs include:

- The ability to accrue points or miles that can be redeemed for free travel (flights, hotel rooms, rental cars, train trips, etc.).
- The ability to keep your preferences in an online travel profile for use with all future trips or stays.
- The ability to obtain preferred status, which can provide a whole new set of benefits including:
  o Faster accrual of points/miles
  o Priority treatment (for example, early boarding of flights or priority check-in and/or late check-out at hotels)

o   Upgrades (for example, flight upgrades to first-class, room upgrades at hotels, or rental car upgrades)

o   Gifts (for example, snacks when you check-in at member hotels)

Make sure you are signed up for the relevant frequent traveler program and use it every time you travel.

126

Points/Miles have quantifiable value

Points or miles that you collect through each of your loyalty programs have real value. Generally speaking, hotel points are the most valuable (in terms of how quickly you can convert paid stays into free stays), followed by airline miles, rental car points, and train miles, respectively.

The value of points and miles can easily be quantified. If an average roundtrip ticket on an airline costs $500 or 25,000 miles; you can estimate the value of an airline mile at 2 cents a mile ($500/25,000). If you earn 5,000 miles for a paid ticket roundtrip to California, that earns you $100 in airline miles (5,000 x .02).

Since they have real value, be sure to treat points and miles as you would real cash. Save them up, spend them wisely, and don't let them expire.

AIR TRAVEL:
TRICKS OF THE TRADE

127

TSA Pre-check is life changing

In these days of atrociously long security lines at the airport, having a Known Traveler Number through the TSA Pre-check or Global Entry program can be hugely beneficial. On a typical day, the standard security line might take an hour or so to get through, while the Pre-check line takes just a few minutes.

The TSA Pre-check program is a program run by the Transportation Security Administration (TSA), that allows you expedited security screening when you are departing from an airport in the United States.

Global Entry is a program run by US Customs and Border Patrol (CBP) that gives you expedited entry into the United States when you are flying in from another country. Global Entry also includes the benefits of TSA Pre-check.

Initial registration for both programs can be done on-line. Upon registration, you'll schedule a face-to-face interview where a government agent explains the benefits of the program. You will receive a number known as a Known Traveler Number, that you will load into your online travel profile with all of your airlines. That number will then automatically be added to any reservation you book with that airline, entitling you to expedited security screening.

Invest the time and effort to register for TSA Pre-check or Global Entry as soon as possible.

Also, whether you are registered for TSA Pre-check or not, you will at times need to choose a security line at the airport. Security lines that include wheelchairs, strollers, the elderly, or families with small children will be slow. Security lines filled with business travelers will be fast. Choose wisely.

128

You should have a travel rhythm and mindset

If you are traveling a lot, it's helpful to develop a travel "rhythm", or process for traveling that you use consistently every time you travel.

If you like to pack the Sunday night before a Monday morning flight for business, make sure you always pack on Sunday night. Pack in the same manner, leave the house at the same time Monday morning, park in the same general location at the airport, load the belt at the x-ray scanner in the same order, grab a coffee or a water if that's your routine, get to the gate at the same time, etc.

Having a travel rhythm will help reduce the anxiety of travel and makes it less likely that you will forget something.

Mindset is also important when you travel. Traveling through the airport is not the time to break out the type-A personality. Invariably there are going to be issues when you travel. Flights will be delayed, connections will be missed, and your fellow passengers will be jerks.

Go into the trip expecting it to not go smoothly, and bring your patience.

129

A full water bottle can be your best friend

It's easy to physically feel under the weather when you travel on an airplane. The combination of the elevation, the motion, the time zone, the cramped quarters, the recycled air, and the stress can combine to make you feel sick.

Hydration plays a large role in how you feel getting off the plane. The elevation and lack of humidity in the cabin air dehydrates you much faster than when you are on the ground. As a result, you need to consume much more water than normal.

Make it a part of your travel routine to buy a bottle of water to bring on the plane. That way you can drink when you're thirsty, you won't be reliant on the flight attendant bringing around the drink cart, and you can consume more water than you'd normally be able to get on the plane. Just remember that you need to buy the water bottle after you get through security; liquids over 3 ounces aren't allowed through airport security.

HOTELS:
FEELING AT HOME

130

You can't sleep where you're not comfortable

There's nothing worse than being in an uncomfortable hotel and not being able to sleep. A hotel room will never feel as comfortable as home, but the more you can do to make it feel like home, the better you'll sleep and the more relaxed you'll feel while you're in it.

After you check in to a hotel, spend the time and effort doing whatever you need to do to make it feel more comfortable. Establish a routine, no matter how silly it is. Check all of the closets, strip the comforter off the bed, untuck the sheets, move the furniture around, adjust the thermostat, look under the bed, empty your luggage and put your clothes in the drawers, open a window, unplug the bright alarm clock, etc.; whatever you need to do to feel more comfortable in the room.

It will be worth it.

131

Hotel room thermostats are important

One problem that can often interfere with your sleep in hotel rooms is the temperature. Figure out what the most comfortable temperature is for you, and always set the hotel thermostat to that exact value. You might find that you want the room a little bit cooler than what you have at home since hotel rooms can often feel hotter and stuffier than your room at home.

Another problem that can often interfere with your sleep in hotel rooms is noise. In addition to road noise, elevator noise, or noise from other guests; the air conditioning unit turning on and off can be very loud.

Setting the thermostat fan to "On" from "Auto", will do two things. One, it will stop the air conditioner fan from constantly cycling on and off, creating that annoying starting and stopping sound. Two, the sound of the fan humming in the background will help drown out other ambient noise.

HOUSES

For most people, their house represents their largest investment. Houses can be expensive and a lot of work to maintain. Here are some things you will need to know as a homeowner in order to keep your house in fine working order.

HOUSE EXPENSES: WHERE MOST OF YOUR MONEY GOES

132

Houses are expensive

Whether you rent an apartment or buy a house or condo, housing is likely to be your largest monthly expense. The rule of thumb is that your monthly housing expense should not exceed 30% of your monthly income before tax, but this is a rough guideline, and many people do spend a higher percentage of their income on housing. What's right for you will depend on your risk tolerance, your income trajectory, your assets, your debts, and frankly the value you place on housing over the other things you can spend your money on.

If you rent, your housing expenses generally consist of rent, utilities, and insurance. If you buy, your housing expenses come in a wider variety of flavors including:

- principal - the amount you borrowed in your mortgage that you have to pay back to the bank
- interest - the amount the bank charges for borrowing the money
- home insurance – the amount you pay to keep insurance on the structure and contents of the house, as well as liability if someone gets hurt on your property
- property tax – the amount that your local government collects as a tax for owning property
- utilities
- maintenance and repair

The first four of these (principal, interest, insurance, and property taxes) are generally paid monthly in one payment to the mortgage company. The mortgage company will then credit your loan by the amount paid to principal, pocket the interest, and put the insurance and property taxes into a holding account known as "escrow." Then they will pay your insurance and taxes out of the escrow account whenever they become due (usually semi-annually). Since the house represents your collateral against the mortgage, the bank has a vested interest in making sure your property taxes and insurance are always paid up-to-date. Collateral means that if you fail to pay your mortgage, the bank can take your house in order to recover what you owe.

In order to determine how much you can afford to spend on housing, there is no shortcut. You will need to analyze your budget to determine how much you are willing to spend in total across principal, interest, insurance, taxes, utilities, and maintenance and repair.

133

It's important to understand how mortgages work

At the end of the day, a mortgage is just a loan. But a mortgage has a few distinct characteristics that make it a special kind of loan. Specifically:

- Since the government promotes home ownership as good for the country, interest paid on a mortgage is generally tax deductible (within certain limits).
- A mortgage is always secured by the property itself, so if the mortgage goes into default (stops being paid), the bank can seize the property.
- Because the mortgage is secured, it has significantly lower risk to the bank than most personal loans. Therefore, they can be very large loans. Because they are very large loans, they also tend to have long terms (timeframes for paying the money back); typically 30 years.
- Since a mortgage is used to purchase real estate, the mortgage amount also ends up being investment "leverage." Leverage is a term that refers to using borrowed money to make money. In terms of a mortgage, it works like this. Let's say you buy a

$250,000 house and pay for it with $50,000 of your own money and $200,000 of the bank's money, obtained as a mortgage. If the value of your house appreciates by 4% a year, you make 4% on the total value of the house ($250,000), not just on the portion that you paid for out-of-pocket ($50,000). This can create substantial wealth when real estate appreciates.

Mortgages come in all sorts of different shapes and sizes. They can vary in term, typically in the 5, 7, 10, 15, or 30-year variety. They can vary in type of rate including fixed rates, where the interest rate stays constant throughout the term of the loan; variable rates, where the interest rate changes on some periodic basis, typically a year; or a hybrid where the rate is fixed for some period of time and then it becomes variable. Then there are other variants including balloons, where the mortgage has a lump-sum payment still due at the end of the term; and interest-only, where your payments don't reduce the principal for a portion of the term. And of course, mortgages also vary in rate and fees.

The decision on which mortgage is right for you can't be answered in this book. It requires research and is dependent upon your risk tolerance, cash-flow situation, available assets, etc. The important thing is to understand the basics of how mortgages work, and what to consider.

HOUSE MAINTENANCE: AN OUNCE OF PREVENTION

134

You can pay for maintenance or pay for the repairs

"An ounce of prevention is worth a pound of cure."

- Benjamin Franklin

The purpose of maintenance is to avoid costly repairs.

When it comes to any kind of preventative maintenance; be it for your house, your car, or anything else; you should consider it required.

135

Houses are a lot of work

Just keeping up with a house is a lot of work. There are no shortcuts; for each of these areas below you will either need to do the work yourself, outsource it directly, or pay for it through a homeowners' association (HOA) or condo fee:

- House Cleaning – The bigger the house, the more the effort (or cost) there will be to keep the house clean. Keeping the house "picked up" is not the same as keeping the house clean. Vacuuming, dusting, and mopping (for example) are required to keep your house in good working order.

- Landscaping – Lawns need to be mowed and flower beds need to be weeded. If you have a small yard, this will still require your time and/or money. Even if you have no yard at all, you may still have landscaping costs to contend with like snow removal for your driveway.

- Pest Control – You may be able to go a period of time without having to deal with pests like insects or rodents. But at some point, it's likely that you will need to deal with ants or mice yourself or through an exterminator. Depending on where you live, you may even need to subscribe to a pest control service to apply preventative measures on an ongoing basis to keep pests out of your house.

136

Houses require seasonal preparation

If you live in a cold weather state, there are several things you need to do late each fall to keep your house in good repair come the spring.

Examples include:

- Turning off the water to outdoor spigots and removing any hoses that are attached (so the house pipes don't freeze and burst)
- If you have an in-ground sprinkler system, paying a sprinkler service to have it blown out with compressed air (so the sprinkler pipes don't freeze and burst)
- Running off the remaining gas in the lawn mower and in other gas-powered outdoor tools used during the summer (otherwise, the gasoline may separate and ruin the engine).
- Cleaning out the gutters (to avoid blockage that can lead to water damage)
- Raking and taking away leaves (so they don't smother your lawn)
- Applying winterizing fertilizer to the lawn (to help it grow back green and lush in the spring)
- Removing window screens

- Sealing drafty windows or doors
- Putting away or tarping patio furniture
- Making sure the snow thrower starts up (because you don't want to find out after the first big snowstorm)
- Cleaning and turning on the whole house humidifier, if you have one
- Replacing the batteries in the smoke detectors

Likewise, there are several things you need to do early each spring to make your house ready for the summer.

Examples include:

- Turning on the water to outdoor spigots and connecting the hoses as appropriate
- Running off the remaining gas in the snow thrower (otherwise, the gasoline may separate and ruin the engine).
- Putting in window screens
- Putting out or removing the tarp from patio furniture
- Making sure the lawn mower starts up (because you don't want to find out when your grass needs to be cut)
- Turning off the whole house humidifier, if you have one
- Replacing the batteries in the smoke detectors

In summary, houses require seasonal preparation.

137

Houses have parts that require periodic replacement

There are a handful of different parts of your house that require periodic replacement. For example:

- Furnace filters need to be replaced approximately every month.
- Smoke detector batteries need to be replaced every six months.
- Roofs need to be replaced every 20 years or so.

Inside your furnace is a replaceable filter that cleans the air of dirt and allergens. This filter gets filthy quickly. When it gets too dirty it starts to impede the airflow through the furnace, which will impact the efficiency of how your house heats up and cools. This filter need to be replaced approximately every month.

Smoke detectors, even those that are hard-wired into the electricity of the house, have batteries as back-up power. The battery in every smoke detector needs to be replaced approximately every six months. An easy way to remember to do it, is to change the batteries whenever the time changes for daylight savings.

A typical asphalt shingle roof needs to be replaced every 20 years or so. In general, this is a job you should hire a professional to do. Roofs can be expensive, so it's good to understand how old your current roof is, so you know approximately when you'll have to pay for a new one. The age of the roof is also an important consideration whenever you buy a house, so you can appropriately price an offer.

The important thing is to remember that some things in your house will need to be periodically replaced.

HOUSE ISSUES: A POUND OF CURE

138

Small problems can become big problems

Just as preventative maintenance can save you from big repairs down the road, taking care of small issues as soon as they pop up can prevent them from becoming big problems. Consider these examples:

- That small leak in the roof can lead to extensive water damage and mold, leading to the need to remove drywall and rotted wall joists.
- That small patch of damaged siding could let in rodents that nest in your attic and require a professional exterminator to get rid of them.
- That ice dam that's formed in the gutter can cause ice and snow to continue to pile up until it rips the gutter from the roof.
- That small crack in the porch can continue to get wider and wider until a large chuck of cement breaks away.
- That small clog in the sink can lead to a major clog deep in the plumbing, require extensive professional plumbing help to resolve.
- That snow and ice that builds up against the house every winter can eventually lead to wet rot, requiring exterior trim to be replaced.

- That occasional insect you see crawling around the kitchen, can easily become an infestation requiring a professional exterminator, or even worse, cause significant structural damage to your house.

In short, if you see a problem fix it right away.

139

It's critical to know where the utility shutoffs are

Your house has main shutoffs for the gas, the electricity, and the water.

When you smell a gas leak, see sparking in an outlet, or have a pipe burst; that is <u>not</u> the time to be figuring out how to shut off the supply to your house.

Make sure you and everyone else in the house knows where the shutoffs are ahead of time, and how to close them by turning them clockwise.

If you do have a significant enough event to require shutting off the main supply to the house, after you shutoff the supply you will probably need to call a professional to fix the issue: the gas company, an electrician, or a plumber.

Also, it should go without saying, but be smart about gas and electricity. If you smell a lot of gas when you enter the house, call the fire department, don't run into the basement to find the gas shutoff. Likewise, if your house is a raging inferno, call the fire department, don't worry about shutting off the electricity.

140

Appliances eventually fail

You're likely to have several large appliances in your house, including a washer, dryer, refrigerator, oven, cooktop, microwave, garbage disposal, dishwasher, air conditioner, hot water tank, microwave, and perhaps some other things.

None of these appliances will last forever. In general, the lifespan of your average appliance ranges from about seven years to twenty years based on the type and quality of the appliance. If you take into account that your house might have 10 or so appliances in it that can break down, that means that every year you are likely dealing with a broken or breaking appliance.

There's no reason to get overly upset when an appliance breaks. It's a normal part of home ownership. There are a few things that you can do to make it less annoying:

- Treat your appliances well and maintain them as recommended. If you are always letting silverware fall into your garbage disposal, it's certainly going to fail faster than if you kept its diet limited to fruit peels and other foodstuffs.
- Budget for appliance repairs or purchases. This is one of those budget items that doesn't come up every month, but when it does come up, it's going to be a big

number. Save a little bit every month for this contingency and it won't put as big a hole in your budget when an appliance fails.

In summary, appliances fail. Don't be surprised and plan ahead.

141

It's important to know what to do after a burglary

A burglary is an awful event that can leave you emotionally vulnerable and frightened. Here is what you do if your discover that your house has been burglarized (or if you have anything stolen in general):

- Call the police and file a police report. You will need this for the insurance company.
- Call the insurance company. They will send out someone (called a claims adjuster) to help you file a claim.
- Remind yourself that life is about loved ones, not about material possessions. Your insurance will reimburse you for your financial losses so that you can replace what was stolen.
- If you feel vulnerable, take steps to make your house more secure going forward; perhaps by having a security system installed, if you don't already have one.

142

You need an emergency preparation plan and kit

Disasters can and do happen unexpectedly. Tornados, earthquakes, floods, hurricanes, and political unrest can cause a temporary breakdown in essential services; often with little to no notice.

You need to have an emergency preparation plan and kit ready for such an occurrence. The US Government provides a good website on this topic, www.ready.gov. Your emergency kit should include the following, at a minimum:

- Three days' worth of water assuming one gallon per day per person. If your house has a hot water tank, this could serve as your emergency water storage, but you will still need enough containers to fill from the tank to provide the required amount if you need to evacuate the house.
- At least a three day supply of non-perishable food.
- Flashlights
- Battery powered radio
- First aid kit
- Extra batteries

There are companies out there that sell premade emergency kits (including freeze dried food). You can easily find one of these companies online. It's worth investing in one of these kits.

In addition to your preparedness kit, you'll also want to have all of your important documents (birth certificates, passports, etc.) as well as some cash in a location that you can easily grab if you need to evacuate the house quickly. A document safe or small firebox works well for this purpose.

In case you do need to quickly evacuate, everyone in the house should be aware ahead of time of the emergency plan; including escape routes, the emergency meeting place, and the location of the emergency kit. If possible, there should be at least two escape routes from every room in the house. For houses with multiple stories, this might necessitate keeping fire escape ladders in upstairs rooms.

Hopefully none of this preparation will be required, but disasters do happen and preparation can save the lives of you and your family.

CARS

Car technology is changing quickly. Who knows what the future holds in the world of driverless electric cars? Presumably, they will still cost money to run, maintain, and repair; and there will still be things you need to know to deal with the unexpected. In any case, as of today here are some things you need to know to keep getting yourself from point A to point B.

CAR EXPENSES: THE PURCHASE IS JUST THE BEGINNING

143

Operating a car is expensive

Cars are expensive to buy and expensive to run. Operating expenses include:

- Insurance
- Gasoline
- Maintenance and Repair

Auto insurance policies are sold in six month terms, and can run hundreds or thousands of dollars per term. Car insurance covers:

- damage to your car if you get in an accident (collision)
- damage to your car if it gets stolen or damaged from something other than an accident (comprehensive)
- damage to other people or their property for accidents that are your fault (liability)
- damage to you, your car, or your passengers when an uninsured or underinsured driver is at fault (uninsured motorist).

Auto Insurance may also include other add-ins, like rental reimbursement and roadside assistance. Auto insurance is required by law.

Selecting an auto insurance policy is largely a question of cost. Generally speaking the cost of your insurance is a function of:

- who you are and where you live. Things like gender, age, and location are used by insurance company actuaries to set the base insurance premiums.
- what you drive. The newer and more expensive the car, the higher the insurance premiums.
- your driving record. The more accidents or traffic tickets you have and the more recent they are, the higher the insurance premiums.
- discounts. Insurance companies offer a litany of different discounts if you are a student, if you don't drive much, or if you have other insurance products with them (like home or renters insurance).

Gasoline varies in price, in general with the cost of oil. Ironically though, the price of gasoline has little impact on America's gasoline consumption. Nonetheless, gas is a very significant expense for car owners today, and as such you should budget for it and be cognizant of it as you consider your driving in financial decisions. If you drive a lot, expect gasoline to eat up hundreds of dollars from your monthly budget.

Maintenance and repair costs are often underestimated in budgets, but you can expect to spend thousands of dollars a year maintaining the car's fluids, tires, brakes, plugs, belts; as well as random repairs that pop up along the way.

In summary, operating a car is expensive!

144

It's worthwhile to understand how a car works

You don't have to be a car expert, but you do need to know the basics of how a car works. Here's why: whenever you take your car to the mechanic for maintenance or repairs, he is going to recommend additional things you should get done. If you don't have some idea how the car works, you won't be able to determine what work you really need to do and what work you can hold off on. Of course, you can and should get the mechanic's opinion; but it's important to recognize that he has his own agenda, he wants to sell as many of his services as possible.

This is hardly exhaustive, and every car is different, but here are some of the basics you need to know (highly simplified):

- The **engine** powers the car by taking a vapor mixture of gasoline and air, igniting it with a spark from the **spark plug**, creating a controlled explosion that moves **pistons** up-and-down, and transfering power through a complicated set of belts and gears to the **axle**(s). When you hear that a car is a V-4 or a V-6, the number refers to the number of pistons, which is related to how much power the car has (and how much fuel it consumes).

- The **transmission** controls the gear ratio to control the power and the speed transferred to the axle(s). Consider how the different gears in your ten-speed bicycle made it easier or harder to pedal. That's what the transmission controls in your car.

- Cars can either be **front-wheel drive, rear-wheel drive, or all-wheel (four wheel) drive.** This refers to which wheels are actually driven by the **drive-train** (the connection to the engine); the other wheels just roll freely. Cars with rear-wheel drive tend to have more power and acceleration (the drive-train pushes the car), while front-wheel cars tend to have more control, especially in slippery conditions (the drive-train pulls the car). Cars with all-wheel drive tend to have the best control since all four wheels touching the ground get power. The trade-off for all-wheel drive is fuel consumption.

- The **brakes** are generally either disk brakes or drum brakes. In both cases they work by applying pressure from a brake pad or shoe against the brake rotor or brake drum that controls the rotational speed of the wheel. Brake pads and shoes wear down and need to be periodically replaced.

- **Tires** need to be rotated (switched around on the car) periodically because the front and back, as well as the left-side and right-side, tires wear differently. Tires also need to be replaced when their tread wears down too far. Tread is measured in 32nds of an inch; new tires start around 10/32; and tires need to be replaced when the tread gets down to 2/32. There is a common rule-of-thumb called the penny test, which is where you put a penny in the tread of the tire, and if the tread is less than the distance from the top of Abraham Lincoln's head to the top of the penny (about 2/32"), you need a new tire.

- Your car uses several different fluids that are required for it to run. **Oil** provides lubrication for the very hot metal parts of the engine that rub together. Oil needs to be replaced relatively frequently. **Coolant** circulates through the engine to keep it from overheating. **Transmission Fluid**, **Brake Fluid**, and **Power Steering Fluid** are used by the transmission, brakes, and steering systems, respectively. **Refrigerant** (Freon) is used in the air conditioning system, and **washer fluid** is used with the windshield wipers.

- Your car also uses several filters that need to be periodically replaced. The **oil filter** removes pollutants from the oil as it circulates through the engine. The **air filter** removes dirt and debris from the air intake that is used to help cool the engine. Lastly, the **cabin filter** removes dust and allergens from the air that blows out into the car as heat or air conditioning.

This book doesn't give you a comprehensive understanding of how a car works, but at least understanding the basics is important.

CAR MAINTENANCE: PROTECTING YOUR INVESTMENT

145

Cars require checkups

Every 7,000 miles or so, cars need to go in for maintenance. The exact schedule differs by make and model; and newer models typically alert you when they need to go in for routine maintenance.

Routine maintenance includes an oil change, and may also include other maintenance items that are on a less frequent schedule including tire rotation, the replacement of other fluids, changing air and cabin filters, etc. While you could certainly do most of this maintenance yourself (it's not that hard), it is typically not economically worthwhile, given that a mechanic has all of the equipment and skills to do the job efficiently.

Part of the maintenance service will likely include a multi-point inspection, where the mechanic will identify needed repairs or additional preventative maintenance. Beware that mechanics will try and sell services that you may not need, or may not need yet. This doesn't make them bad mechanics, it makes them good salespeople. Don't purchase any services that you're not comfortable with, but hear out the mechanic because she is your eyes and ears into the state of your vehicle and only she can tell you if you have a serious issue on your hands. Ask questions, and don't be afraid to tell her no to some or all of her recommendations.

Unless you want to go through the effort of keeping track of what maintenance on your car was done and when it was done, there is benefit to going to the same mechanic for all of your maintenance as they will keep track of all of the work they have ever done on the car. In most cases, they will also have access to recalls that are initiated by the manufacturer.

146

It's worthwhile to know how to jump start your car

Your car battery serves a very specific purpose: it starts your car. The spark from the plugs that ignites the fuel mixture when you turn the key in the ignition is provided by the battery. Once the car is running, the electricity that continues to power the spark plugs, as well as the lights and radio, is generated by the fuel combustion through a device in the car known as the **alternator**. This is why you can actually drive a car with a dead battery, but not start the car. In addition to providing electricity for the car, the alternator is also responsible for keeping the battery charged.

If you do have a dead battery, you'll need to replace the battery, which needs replacing every 5 years or so, or you'll need to jump start the car. In general, always try and jump start the car and recharge the battery before getting it replaced; there is no reason to change out a good battery.

If you have access to jumper cables and a running car, you can easily jump start the car yourself. Otherwise, you can call your insurance company or a local auto club for roadside assistance and pay them to jump start your car. It's worthwhile from both a financial and time perspective to keep jumper cables in your car.

Here are the steps to jump start a car:

- Find someone with a working car and have them park their vehicle next to yours or nose-to-nose with yours.
- Shut off the ignition in the other car.
- Take out the jumper cables and attach a red clip to the positive terminal of your dead battery.
- Attach the other red clip to the positive terminal of the battery in the other car.
- Attach one of the black clips to the negative terminal of the battery in the other car.
- Attach the last black clip to an unpainted metal surface on your car that isn't near the battery (for example, the metal pole that holds the hood open).
- Start the other car.
- Start your car.
- Disconnect the cables in the reverse order in which you connected them.
- Don't turn your car off for at least 15 minutes. This gives the alternator some time to recharge the battery.

147

It's worthwhile to know how to change a tire

Just like with a dead battery, it's worthwhile to know how to deal with a flat tire yourself. Otherwise, you will need to call your insurance company or a local auto club for roadside assistance and pay them to put on your spare.

As long as you are in a relatively safe area, you should not drive the car with a flat tire because it can further damage the tire (perhaps to the point that it can't be repaired). However, if you are in an unsafe area or don't have the room to safely pull over to put on the spare tire, you can drive very slowly on the flat tire until you get to a safe location.

Once you are on level ground in a safe area away from traffic, here is how you change a tire:

- Turn on your hazard lights and apply the parking brake.
- Get the lug wrench, jack, and spare tire out of the trunk of your car. If you're missing any of these three things, you can't go any further, and you'll have to call the insurance company or auto club.
- Using the lug wrench, loosen the lug nuts holding the flat tire by turning them counter-clockwise. They are going to be very tight, so you might need to stomp on the lug wrench to get them started. Don't remove the

nuts at this point. You just want to loosen them while the car is sitting on the ground and not yet up on the jack.

- Put the jack under the car, next to the flat tire and directly under the metal frame of the car (not the plastic molding).

- Use the jack to raise the vehicle until the flat tire is a few inches off the ground. Make sure no part of your body goes under the car. At this point the car is off the ground and can crush you.

- Completely remove the lug nuts by turning them by hand counter-clockwise until they come off.

- Lift the flat tire off of the bolts, and put it in the trunk.

- Put the spare tire onto the bolts.

- Put the lug nuts back on and hand tighten them by turning them clockwise. Don't use the lug wrench yet.

- Use the jack to lower the vehicle to the ground.

- Use the lug wrench to tighten the lug nuts by turning them clockwise.

- Put the jack, lug wrench, and anything else you've taken out back in the trunk.

- Drive the car slowly while you have the spare tire on. The spare is not typically a full tire and will not hold up at freeway speeds or on long trips. It can be dangerous to drive at high speeds or for long distances on a spare tire.

- When convenient, take the car to the mechanic to get the tire fixed or replaced.

CAR ISSUES: WHEN THINGS GO WRONG

148

It's important to know what to do if you get pulled over

If you get pulled over by a police officer for a moving violation, you need to know how to act. Here is what you should do:

- Turn on your hazard lights.
- Look for a safe location to pull over. The location should ideally be to the right of the road, well clear of traffic, and safe both for you and for the police officer who will be getting out of his car and standing next to your car. If you need to drive for a little while to get to a safe location, do so. Your hazard lights and your driving behavior should adequately indicate to the officer that you are looking for a place to pull over.
- Pull over and put the car in park.
- Stay in the car, roll down your window, and if it's dark, turn on your interior lights so that the police officer can see inside the car.
- Keep your hands on the steering wheel in sight of the officer. If you need to take your hands off the wheel to retrieve your license or registration, let him know that's what you are doing. Move slowly and deliberately. Remember that police officers have a dangerous job

which causes them to be in a constant state of alert. You don't want to give them any reason to think that you are a danger to them.

- If you plan on fighting the ticket in court, don't admit guilt.
- Be polite.
- Don't be argumentative. The officer has all of the power in this scenario.
- Be careful when you merge back into traffic.

149

It's important to know what to do if your car breaks down

Cars break down, sometimes at the most inopportune time. Here is what you should do if this happens:

- Turn on your hazard lights.
- Look for a safe location to pull over. The location should ideally be to the right of the road, well clear of traffic, and in a safe area.
- Call a family member to let them know what's going on.
- Call for roadside assistance.

Roadside assistance can be obtained a few different ways:

- You can subscribe to roadside assistance as a part of your auto insurance policy. It typically costs only a few dollars a month and allows you to call their toll free number when you need roadside assistance.
- You can sign up for an auto club (like AAA) that provides roadside assistance along with other services. Like roadside assistance through your insurance company, you need to subscribe for this service ahead

of time, and there is a number to call when you need help.

- In the absence of already having a roadside assistance policy in place, you will need to find a local towing service and pay directly for the tow to the nearest mechanic or mechanic of your choice.

After you've gotten your car towed to the mechanic, you might have a tricky decision to make. Should you get the car repaired, or is it time to replace the car? Of course this is an easy decision it it's a new car, but what if it's near end-of-life? Here are the factors to consider:

- the value of the car (which you can determine from the Kelley Blue Book (www.kbb.com))
- the cost of the repairs
- the cost to replace the car
- the likelihood that more repairs are coming soon

Of course the last consideration is the hardest to determine and perhaps the most influential. If the cost to repair the car is more than what the car is worth, it's clearly time for a new car. However, if you pay to repair the car now and then have another costly repair a month down the road, your car can quickly become a money pit. One shortcut is to consider the cost of the repair in comparison to what your monthly payment would be for a new car. If you compare a monthly car payment of $300/month to a repair costing $600, it's reasonable to determine that if you can get at least two more months out of the vehicle, it's worth it. But you never know.

150

It's important to know what to do after a car accident

Car accidents are scary. If you are unfortunate enough to be in a car accident, here are the steps you need to take:

- If anyone is seriously hurt, dial 911 immediately.
- Turn on your hazard lights.
- Stay at the scene.
- If the accident is minor, move any involved cars to a safe area out of traffic.
- Call the police and get a police report.
- Exchange name, phone number, and insurance information with all involved parties.
- Don't admit guilt.
- If your car can't be driven, call the insurance company, the auto club, or a local towing company for roadside assistance.
- Call your insurance company as soon as you can and report a claim. Your claims adjuster will walk you through everything from there.

THE FULL LIST

MONEY
Personal Finance in a Nutshell
1. Personal finance has four parts
Budgets: The King of Personal Finance
2. A monthly budget is your most important financial tool
3. Creating a monthly budget is easy
4. Your monthly budget should balance
5. You need to budget for savings
6. It's easiest to save the money you never see
7. You will spend what you make
8. Budgets are evergreen
9. You should periodically review recurring payments
Assets and Debts: Two Sides of the Same Coin
10. Assets are thought of in terms of risk and return
11. Debt is neither good nor bad
12. You should consider assets and debts as a portfolio
13. Financial decisions are about balancing risk and return
14. The liquidity of assets varies widely
15. Your credit report matters
Cash Flow: Lubrication to Keep it Running
16. You need multiple checking and saving accounts
17. Business expenses should stay separate
18. Automatic payments are your friend
19. You need mechanisms to manage cash flow
20. Cash flow issues are not necessarily budget issues
21. Balancing your checkbook is a waste of time
22. Auditing your expenses makes sense
Risk Management: Protect for the Unexpected
23. Insurance companies make money
24. Insurance is for catastrophes, not the little stuff
25. You want the largest deductible you can afford
26. Life Insurance is really Salary Insurance
27. Comparing insurance policies can save you thousands
28. Extended warranties are for suckers
29. Fraud happens
30. Anyone can lose their job
Savings: Converting Income to Assets

31. Compound interest is magical
32. Saving for retirement starts now
33. You need short-term savings
34. You need an emergency nest egg account
35. College savings starts at birth
36. Retirement savings takes priority over all others

Investing: Making Your Money Work

37. There are many different types of investments
38. Lending vehicles tend to be low risk and liquid
39. Ownership vehicles create wealth
40. You should take advantage of company stock
41. Professionals should handle the important stuff
42. Diversification is the most important investment strategy
43. Longer timeframes warrant more aggressive investments
44. Panic and exuberance lead to bad decisions

Credit Cards: Friend and Foe

45. It's important to understand how credit cards work
46. Avoiding credit card fees and interest charges is critical
47. Maximizing credit card benefits is smart

Taxes: Uncle Sam's Piece of the Pie

48. It's important to understand how income taxes work
49. Your W-4 is important
50. Tax considerations matter
51. Contributing to a healthcare FSA is free money
52. It's worthwhile to know how to file

Buying vs Renting: The Tradeoffs

53. Many things can be bought or rented
54. In general, buying is better in the long term
55. Renting has its place

Outsourcing: Time is Money

56. Time has value
57. Sometimes, someone else can do it cheaper

CAREER

The Work: Doing It Right

58. Your job is brought to you by your customers
59. Quality is king
60. Time is finite
61. Importance and urgency are different
62. Focus is everything
63. All things are not equally important

64. It's important to always keep the end in mind
65. The Pareto Principle is applicable most of the time
66. It's good to under-promise and over-deliver
67. It only takes one missed commitment to destroy trust
68. Owners beg for forgiveness, not ask for permission
69. You have to enjoy the ride
70. Vacations are required
71. You should embrace change
72. You should always be relevant
73. You should never stop learning
74. It's important to know how to handle a bad role

Your Boss: Becoming Successful Together

75. Bosses and peers need to be managed
76. Your success is tied to your boss' success
77. Surprises suck
78. You should bring solutions, not problems
79. Leaders have different styles
80. Employees must adapt upward
81. Outworking your boss sends a good message
82. Bosses love initiative
83. Receiving feedback is an important skill

Managing Expectations: Baselines Matter

84. Success is always measured as results against expectations
85. All business is show business
86. Perception often is reality
87. Expectations need to be managed early and often

The Workplace: Keeping it Professional

88. Companies have personalities
89. You should dress for the job you want
90. When in doubt, you should over-dress
91. After-hours work events are still work events

Professional Relationships: Required for Success

92. Networking is a part of the job
93. Remembering names matters
94. You should always be genuine
95. Diversity has a population of one
96. The Golden Rule is wrong
97. Roles change suddenly

Communication: The Life-Blood of Business

98. Work is a team sport
99. In terms of collaboration, one plus one equals three

100. Collaboration can save your job
101. You need to learn to read people
102. How you communicate matters
103. It's usually best to listen first and speak second
104. Active listening is a skill
105. Crisp is clear

Negotiation: Science, not Art
106. Negotiation is a skill
107. You should always seek to understand "why"
108. It's important to find common ground
109. Balance of power matters
110. You need to understand your BATNA

Management and Leadership: It's About People
111. Leaders have followers
112. All people are intrinsically motivated by the same things
113. Responsibilities should be delegated; not tasks
114. Only the committed can commit
115. Great leaders are like umbrellas
116. All volunteers are good volunteers
117. Giving feedback is an important skill

Job Security: Your Job, Your Problem
118. Job security is not the responsibility of your employer
119. Job security is a function of your value to the company
120. Job security is a function of your value to the market
121. Job security is a function of your network
122. Your résumé should always be up to date
123. There is a right way to quit
124. There is a right time to quit

TRAVEL
Travel Rewards: Membership has its Privileges
125. It's worthwhile to register for loyalty programs
126. Points/Miles have quantifiable value

Air Travel: Tricks of the Trade
127. TSA Pre-check is life changing
128. You should have a travel rhythm and mindset
129. A full water bottle can be your best friend

Hotels: Feeling at Home
130. You can't sleep where you're not comfortable
131. Hotel room thermostats are important

HOUSES
House Expenses: Where Most of Your Money Goes
132. Houses are expensive
133. It's important to understand how mortgages work
House Maintenance: An Ounce of Prevention
134. You can pay for maintenance or pay for the repairs
135. Houses are a lot of work
136. Houses require seasonal preparation
137. Houses have parts that require periodic replacement
House Issues: A Pound of Cure
138. Small problems can become big problems
139. It's critical to know where the utility shutoffs are
140. Appliances eventually fail
141. It's important to know what to do after a burglary
142. You need an emergency preparation plan and kit

CARS
Car Expenses: The Purchase is Just the Beginning
143. Operating a car is expensive
144. It's worthwhile to understand how a car works
Car Maintenance: Protecting your Investment
145. Cars require checkups
146. It's worthwhile to know how to jump start your car
147. It's worthwhile to know how to change a tire
Car Issues: When Things Go Wrong
148. It's important to know what to do if you get pulled over
149. It's important to know what to do if your car breaks down
150. It's important to know what to do after a car accident

ACKNOWLEDGMENTS

Special thanks to Suzanne Cornelius and Kristen Cornelius for editing support; and to Brad Fagan for support with design and formatting.

INDEX

1040 98

401(k) 62, 69

50/50 rule 21

529 plan 66, 96

80/20 rule 117

active listening 141, 168

adapting upward 137

air filter 237

air travel 200

airline miles 197

airport security 201

Albert Einstein 60

allowance 37

all-wheel drive 236

alternator 241

Antoine de Saint-Exupery 179

Apple 74

appliances 226

Arthur Andersen 57

ask for permission 121

assets 14, 25, 26, 30

attire 150, 151

auditing 44

auto club 248

automatic payments 39, 89

automatic transfers 20, 37, 64

automobile 231

accident 250

break down 248

expenses 232

issues 245

maintenance 238

autonomy 178, 179

axle 235

balance sheet 13

BATNA 175

beg for forgiveness 121

Benjamin Franklin 216

Blockbuster 57

bonds 26, 71, 81

bonus 21

Borders Books 57

bosses 131

brake fluid 237

brakes 236

budget 14, 15, 42

burglary 228

business expenses 38

buy low, sell high 84

buying 99

cabin filter 237

cable TV providers 24

career 107

cars .... see automobile

cash flow 14, 35, 37, 40, 42, 43

certificates of deposit 71

change, dealing with 124

changing a tire 243

checkbook 43

checking account ... 20, 36, 38, 39, 64

closing costs 103

coinsurance 52
collaboration 163, 164
collectibles 71
college savings 66
commitment 180
commodities 71
communication 161
company culture 149
coolant 237
cost basis 78
credit cards 14, 38, 40, 55, 85
benefits 90
credit report 34
crisp communication 169
customer experience 144
customers 109
Dan Millman 124
Daniel Pink 178
day trading 84
debt 14, 25, 28, 30, 32
delegation 179
diversify 75, 81, 82
diversity 157
diversity of one 157
dollar-cost averaging 68
Dwight D. Eisenhower 113
earthquakes 229
electricity providers 24
emergency nest egg account 65
emergency preparation 229
Employee Stock Purchase Plan 78
engine 235
enjoying work 122
Enron 57, 78
escrow 212

ESPP 78
expectations 142, 143, 147
extended warranties 54
extrinsic motivation 178
exuberance 84
FDIC 72
Federal Deposit Insurance
Corporation 72
fees 41, 86, 88, 93, 94
financial aid 67, 69
financial catastrophe 48, 51, 65
financial frame-of-reference 22
financial planning 16
financial timeframes 83
floods 229
focus 114
followers 177
four-wheel drive 236
fraud 44, 55
free money 62, 66, 78, 97
front-wheel drive 236
furnace filters 220
gas providers 24
genuine 156
giving feedback 183
Global Entry 201
Golden Rule 158
Health Savings Account 97
HOA 217
home repairs 216, 223
homeowners' association 217
hotel points 197
hotels 205
house cleaning 217
house expenses 210

house issues.............................. 222

house maintenance.................. 215

houses 209, 211

hurricanes 229

hydration................................. 204

identity theft........................34, 56

impact...................................... 187

importance 113, 114, 115, 132

income statement..................... 13

initiative 139

insurance............... 14, 24, 46, 211

    auto...............46, 233, 243, 248

    dental...............................46, 52

    disability.............................. 47

    health..............................46, 52

    home 46, 211

    liability................................. 46

    life....................................46, 51

    renter's 46

    vision...............................46, 52

insurance deductibles.......... 50, 52

insurance premiums.....46, 50, 52, 234

integrity.................................... 110

interest 26, 60

    credit card interest.............. 86

    loan interest....... 30, 32, 34, 41

    mortgage interest.......211, 213

internet providers..................... 24

intrinsic motivation................. 178

investment....................26, 68, 70

job security.............................. 185

job, losing a 57, 65

Johann Wolfgang von Goethe
.... 114

jump start, automobile 241

keeping the end in mind......... 116

Kelley Blue Book 249

Known Traveler Number...... 201

landscaping............................. 217

leaders vs managers................ 177

leadership................................ 176

leadership styles...............136, 177

learning 128

lending vehicles 71

leverage 28, 75, 213

LinkedIn 154, 190

liquidity 33, 72

listening............................167, 168

loyalty programs 197

management............................. 176

managers vs leaders................ 177

Mary Parker Follett............... 172

mastery.................................... 178

micro-management................. 179

mobile providers 24

money...................................... 11

money market accounts 71

mortgage................... 96, 211, 213

motivation 178

moving violation 246

multi-point inspection 239

mutual funds 71

names 155

natural disasters 229

negotiation.......................170, 171

    finding common ground.. 173

    power 174

    understanding why........... 172

net worth 14

oil 237
oil change 239
oil filter 237
online tools 18
opportunity cost 105
outsourcing 104, 105, 106
over-deliver 119
overdraft 40
owners vs workers 121
ownership vehicles 71, 74
panic 84
Pareto Principle 117
passion 182
penny test 236
perception as reality 145
performance feedback 140
personal finance 12
pest control 217
pistons 235
political unrest 229
portfolio 30, 81, 89
power steering fluid 237
preferred status 197
principal 211
professional money managers 75, 80
professional networking . 154, 189
professional relationships 153
pulled over 246
purpose 178
quality 111
quarterly reviews 23, 24
quitting 191, 193
raise 21
reading people 165

real estate 71, 74, 213
rear-wheel drive 236
receiving feedback 140
recurring payments 24
refrigerant 237
relevance 126, 187, 188
renting 99
reputation 119, 152
résumé 190
retirement 62, 68, 83, 96
return 26, 31, 60, 74, 80, 81, 83, 89
risk 26, 31, 72, 74, 80, 81, 83
risk management 14, 45
roadside assistance 248
Roger Fisher 175
role 159
    bad role 129
roofs 220
Roth 62, 96
rule of 70 60
savings 20, 59
savings account 36
savings account . 20, 26, 40, 64, 71
self-insured 48
severance 65
sewer providers 24
Shel Silverstein 122
sleep 206
smoke detectors 220
Social Security 63
solutions, not problems 135
spark plug 235
spending 16
Start, Stop, Continue 141

statement of cash flows............ 13
stock.................26, 71, 74, 77, 81
stock grants 77
stock options............................. 77
surprises.................................... 134
tax 66, 68, 73, 75, 78, 91
   filing 98
   property taxes 211
tax deductible.....................96, 213
tax deferred 62
tax refund 92, 94
Teddy Roosevelt...................... 135
thermostats............................... 207
time, value of ..104, 105, 112, 114
tire rotation 239
tires... 236
to-do list.................................... 112
tornados.................................... 229
training...................................... 128
transmission 236
transmission fluid.................... 237
Transportation Security
   Administration 201
travel.. 195
travel rewards........................... 196

travel rhythm............................ 203
trust 120
TSA Pre-check........................ 201
TurboTax 98
umbrella leadership................. 181
under-promise 119
urgency...................................... 113
US Customs and Border Patrol
.... 201
utilities.................................24, 211
utility shutoffs.......................... 225
vacation..................................... 123
Vilfredo Pareto 117
volunteers 182
W-4.......................................93, 94
washer fluid.............................. 237
water providers.......................... 24
wealth creation....................74, 77
William Ury 175
windfall 21
work 108
work events............................... 152
workers vs owners 121
workplace 148

ABOUT THE AUTHOR

Shawn Cornelius has spent over 20 years as a management consultant, husband, and father. As a management consultant at Andersen Consulting / Accenture and Rosetta / SapientRazorfish, Shawn has developed a deep passion for the consulting culture of stewardship and teaching. Shawn is also on the Board of Directors for The Centers for Families and Children, a non-profit focused on helping families overcome the barriers of poverty.

Outside of work and philanthropy, Shawn enjoys spending time with his wife and three children, who keep him young with their fresh perspectives on the world. As time permits, Shawn attempts (poorly) to continue playing soccer.

Made in the USA
Columbia, SC
19 December 2019